Sharing Words

Sharing Words

Theory and Practice
of Dialogic Learning

Ramón Flecha

ROWMAN & LITTLEFIELD PUBLISHERS, INC.
Lanham • Boulder • New York • Oxford

AHQ4880

ROWMAN & LITTLEFIELD PUBLISHERS, INC.

Published in the United States of America
by Rowman & Littlefield Publishers, Inc.
4720 Boston Way, Lanham, Maryland 20706
http://www.rowmanlittlefield.com

12 Hid's Copse Road
Cumnor Hill, Oxford OX2 9JJ, England

Copyright © 2000 by Rowman & Littlefield Publishers, Inc.

British Library Cataloguing in Publication Information Available

Library of Congress Cataloging-in-Publication Data

Flecha, Ramón.
    [Compartiendo palabras. English]
    Sharing words : theory and practice of dialogic learning.
        p.   cm.—(Critical perspectives series)
    Includes bibliographical references and index.
    ISBN 0-8476-9595-6 (cloth : alk. paper)—ISBN 0-8476-9596-4 (paper : alk.
paper)
        1. Learning—Social aspects.   2. Critical pedagogy.   3. Dialogue.
    4. Group reading.   5. Communication in education.   I. Title.   II. Series.
    LB1060.F59 ~1999~ 2000
    370.15′23—dc21   99-046275

Printed in the United States of America

∞ ™ The paper used in this publication meets the minimum requirements of
American National Standard for Information Sciences—Permanence of Paper for
Printed Library Materials, ANSI Z39.48–1992.

To the three hundred literary circle participants

Contents

Preface   ix

Introduction: Principles of Dialogic Learning   1

1. Manuel: A Life Spent Struggling against Cultural Inequalities   31

2. Lola: From "Illiterate" to Creator of a Literary Circle   47

3. Chelo: Subject of Her Own Transformation   65

4. Rocío: Overcoming Ageism   79

5. Juan: Decolonizing Everyday Life   91

6. Rosalía: Dialogic Research   103

7. Antonio: Gypsy Contribution to the Dialogue   113

Index   129

About the Author   134

Preface

These pages narrate the story of a *tertulia*, a literary circle, created by adults who were attending basic literacy and new reader classes. Their dialogic learning process led them from a point at which they read no books at all to a point at which they enjoyed the works of Lorca, Kafka, Dostoyevsky, and Joyce. That is the more academic aspect of the transformational process affecting all of their relationships—work-related, social, family, and affective.

None of the three hundred people who participated in this activity had taken part in any university study. None of them were members of that sector of society targeted by most cultural offerings. This literary gathering was designed, we could say, by and for people whom society has considered to be unmotivated by literature.

The dialogues take place in the La Verneda–Sant Martí adult education center, which has been working dialogically for twenty years. The organization was founded as a result of popular movements in a working-class neighborhood in Barcelona. Together with other collectives in the area, it has transformed the urban, cultural, and communitarian landscapes, creating various networks of solidarity and well-being.

Ideally, this book will generate some new ideas or feelings among people who know that non-university-educated members of society have much to offer to the cultural panorama. This study has been written with these people in mind, as well as relatives, friends, and professionals who want to help overturn the educational exclusion of such sectors of society.

Those who wish to carry out an existential reading may wish to skip the introduction or leave it until the very end. In the seven chapters of the book you will find personal sentiments, social theories, and literary knowledge as experienced by the project participants. Life and literature are not divided into separate categories, nor are theories and feelings: in the same way, life and literature, theories and feelings remain undivided in the group discussions.

Those who propose to undertake an analytical reading should begin with the introduction, where the seven principles of dialogic learning are explained, with examples of their relation to the daily activities of the group members. In the remainder of the book, you will find the components necessary for reflection, which may enable this learning experience to be re-created in other contexts.

Introduction

Principles of Dialogic Learning

D ialogic learning requires both abstract explanations and personal accounts. The explanations help both to establish and debate the ideas supporting it. The personalization enables us to see how dialogic learning is experienced on a daily basis. This book brings both of those elements together: the book is a narration through seven chapters that are theorized in this introduction or, if you prefer, a theory first explained in the introduction and exemplified later in the chapters.

The seven principles of dialogic learning endeavor to provide a guide for implementation and reflection. They are all developed throughout the text, although each one is also the focus of one specific chapter: egalitarian dialogue (Manuel), cultural intelligence (Lola), transformation (Chelo), instrumental dimension (Rocío), creating meaning (Juan), solidarity (Rosalía), and equality of differences (Antonio).

The introduction develops each principle in two directions: theoretical explanation of the principle; and concrete examples from the literary circle. The first gathers together the theoretical elements of this type of learning, including the main bibliographical references. The second presents some aspects of its concretion in the literary circle.

This introduction presents the synthesis of a theory that is fully developed in the rest of the book. Chapter by chapter, you will find its constitutive elements, its links to praxis, and its relationship to the other theories and processes through which it is generated.

I believe that dialogic learning is universal, that is, partially valid within many educational situations and contexts, from infancy to old age. Those of you who live these situations should be the ones to decide on their suitability, and you are the only ones who can recreate them.

EGALITARIAN DIALOGUE

A dialogue is egalitarian when it takes different contributions into consideration according to the validity of their reasoning, instead of according to the positions of power held by those who make the contributions.

When a teacher imposes what he or she sees as truth under threat of failure for those who reject it, students are confined by the walls of what is established as correct by authority; the teacher learns nothing, simply repeating what she or he already knows or takes to be true. In egalitarian dialogue both students and teachers learn, since they all construct interpretations based on the contributions made. Nothing can be taken as definitively concluded, as assertions will always be subject to future analysis.[1]

Within the fields of education and social sciences, more and more studies are being carried out along these lines. Habermas's theory of communicative action[2] helps point out ways to organize human relations around dialogue and consensus. Freire's studies[3] show how to fight for egalitarian dialogue within situations of inequality. Beck and Giddens's contributions[4] help develop transformative practices and perspectives directed by people's own reflections.

This dynamic is becoming increasingly feasible through the evolution of contemporary society.[5] Information selection and processing (in the broad sense) are becoming the keys to coping. Egalitarian and reflexive dialogue develops these capacities more firmly than traditional forms of education.

Communicative action theory provides many ways to think about dialogic learning. In my opinion, there are some holes in the theory, particularly within educational topics, which suggest the necessity of avoiding its mechanical application to the question of learning. We adjust its developmental vision because it runs the risk of reducing the diversity and globality of human evolution to a typical Western, schooled childhood and adolescence (thereby excluding both adults and people from other backgrounds).

An expert on Piaget, Habermas has hardly taken into account sociocultural approaches like Vygotsky's,[6] which are important to concepts of dialogic learning. Habermas's latest proposal, though, is more multicultural than his theory of communicative action.[7]

The theory of communicative action's contributions are fundamental, if reexamined from this critical standpoint. The theory helps to rethink educational relationships by clarifying the differences between four types of action: teleological (with a strategic variant), normatively regulated, dramaturgical, and communicative.

In teleological action, a person chooses the best means to reach an end (for example, a teacher wants to teach a class literature and elaborates the best plan to do so). The main concept is the choice between alternative actions (masterfully explaining the literary tendencies, making the students read the texts, or pursuing other possibilities). Language is conceived of as a means like any other to reach the objective (convincing the students of the importance of the suggested readings). The strategic variant is that the instructor keeps in mind the likely aims of each student (if the main objective is to pass a college entrance exam, the teacher will integrate his or her plan with the demands of the exam). Since Aristotle, the teleological has been the predominant concept of action. The strategic variant is found in decision theory, game theory, sociology, and social psychology.

In normatively regulated action, teacher and student are not solitary actors but members of a group who act in accordance with common values (for example, accepting the importance of academic knowledge). The central concept is that of observing a norm leading to the fulfillment of generalized behavioral expectations in accordance with different roles (the student expects the teacher to clarify the meaning of readings). Language here is seen as a means of transmitting dominant values. Durkheim[8] and Parsons[9] developed this normative action model within sociological theory.

In dramaturgical action, participants perform before an audience made up of the rest of the group (the teacher may, say, play the part of the non-comprehended writer for the students). The central concept is that of presentation of self, which consists of a performance being put on for the public (the role of the non-comprehended writer may increase personal interest or respect for the instructor). Language is here converted into the means of presenting the self. Goffman[10] has worked with the sociological conception of this type of action.

Communicative action refers to an interaction in which subjects capable of speech and action enter into an interpersonal relationship using verbal and nonverbal means (one might posit that all people, including the student body and the community, take part in designing their own learning). The central concept is that of interpretation, as related to the negotiation of situations open to consensus (the meanings of texts are established by reasoning and not by the teacher). Language takes a fundamental place as the means of reaching understanding. The communicative action concept has been part of Mead[11] and Garfinkel's work;[12] Habermas also takes into consideration Wittgenstein's language-games,[13] Austin's speech-act theory,[14] and Gadamer's hermeneutics.[15]

The *tertulia*, or literary circle, meets for two hours every week. Together the group chooses a book to read and to discuss during the next session. Everybody reads, reflects, and talks with family and friends over the course of the week. Each person chooses a passage to read aloud and explain why it was particularly meaningful to him or her. The dialogue constructed is then based on these contributions. Different opinions are debated and resolved through discussion. If the entire group reaches an agreement, this is established as a provisionally true interpretation. If consensus is not reached, all the members of the group or subgroup maintain their own positions; no one determines the correct or incorrect reading based on his or her position of power.

The "coordinator" (Goyo) learns as much as, or more than, the "students." Even when he is very sure of something, he cannot impose it but must try to convince the rest of the group. He is, thus, obliged to think and rethink what he previously took for granted, find more reasons to support his opinion, or discover that he was partially or entirely wrong. We see an example of this last possibility, for example, in his debate with Manuel about the importance of correct spelling.

People who hold no academic degrees find new self-esteem upon realizing that they can teach the teacher something and that they can learn a lot by talking among themselves. Suddenly, they stop being passive receptors of knowledge and begin actively to generate knowledge. Reading and reflection become deeper once people realize that the group values their contributions. Manuel's interpretations of Miguel Hernández's poetry both enrich and move the entire group. Manuel's vision differs from the analyses of academic authorities on the subject; it supposes a new creation whose knowledge improves his self-image and increases his willingness to carry out new readings.

The egalitarian dialogue adopted in this exercise is in line with communicative action and differs from teleological, norm-regulated, and dramaturgical action. The teleological action model would have resulted in the teacher (Goyo) elaborating a literary circle for people with a low level of education. The educator would proceed as the lone actor in an objective world; the rest of the participants would be reduced to the status of objects, and the action would be developed without their input. Everything would be designed to achieve the goal: that the group learn literature. Language would not be dialogic or participatory, but a means like any other through which the subject might reach the goal. With the strategic variant, Goyo would have kept in mind, say, that some people wanted to read books that family members with a higher academic level had enjoyed.

The normative model would have led the participants to act in "teacher–student" roles. Goyo would have to present the course guidelines, explain the most important aspects, emphasize the right interpretations, and correct people's errors.

If he envisioned the circle as a site of dramaturgical action, the coordinator would create the images of himself that best enabled him to achieve his objectives. For example, he could play the role of the enthusiastic listener to all of the participants' comments, even when they seemed to him incorrect; he would thus boost participants' self-images and boost their learning. In this instance, language would serve as a way of dramatizing.

Participants like Manuel would reject any activity designed in those terms; they would fight to transform it or else would give up. When they understand that they are able to create their own literary circle, however, they lead it in the form of a dialogue, in step with communicative action. Each person makes individual contributions to the dialogue. The various comments are not classified as better or worse, but are appreciated as different. This horizontality brings the participants closer to an ideal speech situation. Their relationship is simultaneously real and ideal; real because the greater influence of some voices is a reminder that conversation takes place in an unequal context; ideal because it makes headway towards moving beyond inequalities. At first, for example, males and people with more education carried more weight when they made assessments. As the discussions progressed, different commentaries began to be valued more for what they contributed to each participant's readings than for the gender or education of those who provided them.

Within the group, Manuel's contributions constantly relate to the fairness of dialogue. His radicalism seeks to overcome the inequalities found in politics, workers' organizations, businesses, and adult education centers. He has endeavored all his life to prevent the exclusion of the majority of humanity from dialogue. In both political and educational settings he makes the richness of his oral culture felt; he shows that a person or group's voice should always be heard, regardless of lack of purchasing power or educational opportunities.

CULTURAL INTELLIGENCE

Everyone is capable of participating in egalitarian dialogue, although each person may demonstrate his or her ability in different environments. Those who perform well in the market or the factory may feel completely inhibited in the classroom; those who feel at ease in an academic milieu may be be unable to participate adequately at a neighborhood association meeting or in a discotheque. Girls who cannot speak, see, or hear develop rich communicative skills through other forms of expression; shy boys may be quite talkative in certain concrete situations.

In social assessment, privileged groups designate their own forms of communication as intelligent and those of other groups as deficient. In spite of the many proofs of its arbitrary nature, this classification still pervades school evaluations and activities. In this way, theories analyzing supposed shortcomings are projected onto all members of the student body who differ from the young, Western, white, male prototype, that is, these theories are projected onto the majority of the world population.

Among the abundant research that has transcended this conception, I should highlight that which has differentiated between fluid and crystallized intelligence[16] and between academic and practical intelligence.[17] Its great merit has been to give scientific status to something quite obvious: that people considered slow in academic environments may demonstrate great ability in work or family contexts and vice versa. These perspectives are, however, excessively reductive in considering solely the cognitive dimension, based on teleological action.

Dialogic learning requires another, wider conceptualization that looks at the multidimensionality of human interaction and is itself based on egalitarian dialogue.

The Center for Social and Educational Research, CREA (Universitat de Barcelona) works with the concept of cultural intelligence, which considers the totality of human interaction.[18] Among the subsets are academic and practical intelligence and other abilities related to the language and actions of human beings that make it possible to reach agreement in different social situations. Both types of intelligence (academic and practical) presuppose a solitary actor who sets out objectives for him- or herself and chooses the best means to achieve them (teleological action). Cultural intelligence presupposes an interaction whereby different people enter into a relationship that is both verbal and nonverbal (communicative action). In this way they reach cognitive, ethical, aesthetic, and affective understandings.

Communicative abilities are important components of cultural intelligence. Through the use of these abilities many operations, which cannot be resolved by a solitary actor through academic or practical intelligence, can reach resolution. When we buy a washing machine or get a new computer in the office, few of us really learn how it works just by reading the instruction manual. Most of us ask the installer which setting to use for delicates or how to use the virus protection program. According to the dialogical perspective of cultural intelligence, mental operations characteristic of academic and practical intelligence should be analyzed in communicative contexts.

Everyone has cultural intelligence; the inequality is generated by varying development in different environments. Some of us perform well on mechanics exams, others know how to fix the car when it breaks down on the road. A transfer from one area to the other (from the classroom to the road or vice versa) can be made as long as certain conditions are met. The main one is that both the person involved and those who interact with her or him must be convinced that she or he can do it, and that she or he must be given the opportunity to prove this.

It is sometimes said that scholastic skills are abstract, formal, and transferable to other functional settings, but that the reverse is not true. We therefore find that those who have developed technical or social skills often have little confidence in their ability to acquire academic skills. In order for people to gain the self-confidence necessary to learn, ideas of nontransferability must be replaced by other, already well-demonstrated alternatives. All skills are functional within their own contexts and are transferable to others in certain situations. Scholastic abilities are not automatically applicable to other settings, and technical or family-related skills are not necessarily incapable of transfer to the classroom.

The concept of cultural intelligence offers an adequate framework for moving beyond all of the deficit theories, including those specifically dealing with the adult population. Two of these have been of the utmost importance: the quantitative studies maintaining that intelligence declined after youth; and the theories of childhood development as they were applied to adults.

Wechsler[19] and other writers measured the relationship of intelligence to age and concluded that intelligence decreased during adulthood. The mistakes in this type of research are obvious, even from these researchers' own quantitative focus. For instance, these researchers confused age and generation. Their transverse tests measured the intelligence of different people at the same point in time. The results they obtained were attributed to age, although they should have been able to see that each generation had greatly differing learning opportunities. The curves that indicated the decrease in intelligence coincided with those that showed the difference in years of schooling received by each generation. Later longitudinal studies[20] moved beyond this ageist[21] prejudice of science. Instead of comparing the intelligence of different people at the same time, they analyzed the cognitive evolution of the same people throughout their lives. The results showed that intelligence grew or could grow throughout adulthood.

Another ageist concept in cognitive evolution came from the improper application of Piaget's theory.[22] The Swiss psychologist investigated pre-adult cognitive development only. Irresponsible researchers then took the developmental periods of childhood and adolescence that their mentor had researched, and they applied them to adulthood. One of their incorrect conclusions was this: adults who have not finished their obligatory schooling by the "appropriate age" are still in the period of concrete operations. In other words, they are either children who need to develop intellectually or deficient adults who have already missed the boat. What is not taken into account is the training and development such adults have acquired in nonscholastic contexts.

It was Freire who pointed out that these adults have different, not inferior, cognitive abilities. Following the transcultural approach of Vygotsky,[23] Sylvia Scribner[24] showed that adults, in their everyday activities, carry out cognitive operations equivalent to those developed in school during childhood and adolescence. The concept of cultural intelligence combines all of these contributions within the framework of egalitarian dialogue, confirming that all people of all ages possess skills involving language and action that can be developed through their interactions.

All groups have the cultural intelligence to move beyond the classist, racist, sexist, or ageist discrimination that tends to exclude them. Human relations tend towards dialogue, yet they also put up the barriers that impede it. We are constantly developing ways to open up new sources of communication while at the same time hindering others. Information technology has made it possible for us to be connected to any part of the world, but we have also stopped looking at our dinner companions in order to stare at a screen. Education systems have facilitated access to a minimal universal culture, but they have also written off hundreds of millions of people as uncultured and created the stereotype of their lack of ability.

The principal barriers impeding dialogue can be classified into three types:

- Cultural: most members of the population are dismissed as incapable of communicating with each other using dominant knowledge. A select minority formulates theories about the shortcomings of the rest in order to dissuade society as a whole from trying to take cultural center stage.
- Social: many groups are excluded from the production and evaluation of valuable knowledge. Classism, sexism, racism, and ageism confine educational experiences within the bounds of social position, gender, ethnicity, and age; experiences that do not fit the mold are excluded.
- Personal: these keep many people from enjoying the cultural richness of their environment. Many people's personal histories and, especially, the ways they report these histories to one another lead to self-exclusion from many formative practices.

The increasingly frequent changes in personal and collective situations facilitate the dismantling of these barriers. A woman whose separation from her husband drives her to look for a job and make new relationships may feel that her lack of schooling and insecurity are insurmountable barriers. If she takes the step of signing up at an education center, it is important that she makes headway from the first day, finding that she knows more than she thought, that she is going to learn much more and meet interesting people. A good egalitarian dialogue can provide an appropriate atmosphere for initiating her new adventure in life.

In stable situations, the difficulties presented by these barriers do not tend to be so acutely felt, since we generally adapt ourselves to a limited environment. Sometimes, however, our conformity hides negative thoughts about our own ability to improve our lives. Good communication is, in these cases as well, the ideal setting to facilitate the desired transformations.

This book shows how egalitarian dialogue arouses the intellects of people participating in the literary circle. Previously, the participants were all highly skilled within different environments: they were dressmakers, mechanics, homeworkers, bricklayers, mothers, and fathers. At first, all of their self-confidence and creativity tended to turn into inhibition in an academic space. In order to transfer their previous skills to the new setting, we followed a process that can be systematized in three fundamental steps:

- Interactive Self-Confidence: recognition by the group (in formal "class" time) of the important skills already proven in other areas. The members talk about how well they can make change in the market, get over a family conflict and return to harmonious coexistence, or organize a search for a job. The group members talk about texts like García Lorca's praise of the kind of folk creativity that can come up with a name such as "heaven fat" (*tocino de cielo*) to designate a type of candy. Alongside the skills of people who cannot read we see the ignorance of a coordinator who cannot distinguish a pine from an oak. In another meeting, the collective creates self-confidence by rejecting incorrect commentary made by a literature student regarding *Don Quixote*.
- Cultural Transference: discovery of the possibility of demonstrating cultural intelligence in the new academic context. The oral culture used in the market or at lunch also proves valid for the readings, creating penetrating literary analyses. The process Lola went through in order to participate in settings that she would previously have shunned adds great richness to her analysis of works like *The House of Bernarda Alba*. The pedagogical listening frequently practiced by Goyo encourages this transference.
- Dialogic Creativity: confirmation of learning generated by participants' contributions. The various interpretations given are in many cases different from everything previously written on the topic. Thus, not only does literature reach a new public but the public also transforms the readings, enriching them with new ways of bringing them to

life. Lola's comments on *Gypsy Ballads*, for example, differ greatly from what we hear in most literature classes or read in books of literary criticism.

The worst possible behavior, the one that makes advances most difficult, is that of disdain on the part of pseudointellectuals, like those who protest at Mariana's intervention. The best behavior is that of Habermas, publicly recognizing the importance of her question and thereby discrediting those who undervalue her participation in the group.

Interaction at the adult education center fosters the self-confidence that Lola already had in her knowledge. Transference is encouraged by the collective appraisal of the key knowledge she had acquired through oral communication. Dialogic creativity is reflected in examples like the conversation about ballads or "romances" (a type of narrative written in verse), where Lola shows Goyo that defining them is of little use unless you can recite and sing them.

Egalitarian dialogue helps us jump over cultural barriers. Listening to Lola speak about Lorca, we see how deficit theories are continuously refuted in day-to-day practice, clashing with those that view reality from an academic ivory tower. People who at first think they are incapable of understanding classics begin discovering that not only do they understand them, they also provide new interpretations. They then feel able to participate in the process of literary learning. They realize that the more similar their dialogues are to the informal conversations of their childhood, the more instructive they are; the coordinator also realizes that he should use the model of the worker's mule cart or the open space of a troubadour, instead of the models used in the classrooms in which he was trained.

Getting around the social barriers imposed by classism is more of a struggle. The literary circle enables its members to partake of some of the knowledge traditionally reserved for wealthy sectors of society, but not to gain access to most of their cultural spaces. That step requires the coordination of diverse social movements questioning the power base that establishes the sway of a select few over the majority.

Other social barriers are weakened or disappear, making room for everyone's creativity. Lola and other women have to overcome obstacles in order to participate and, as they begin to feel more secure about their training, they overcome, in part, the exclusion they suffer in both job-related and family settings. At the gatherings there are no racist commentaries against groups or individuals. But the foundation of their education is white, male, and Western, that is, conditioned by the way dominant society imposes as universal the literature produced by itself. The walls created by ageism are torn down; the very existence of the group meeting belies the closed category of appropriate activities and extent of learning possible for every age.

Egalitarian dialogue overcomes personal barriers as well. Leaving the house and making one's own friends outside the home, daring to speak in public, feeling secure in a familial or social conversation about cultural topics, or realizing that there is still time to do almost everything are some of the new adventures that some people begin at twenty, fifty, or eighty years of age. In order to open these doors, people must not only overcome their internalized sexist, racist, and ageist assumptions, but also overcome their own shyness, complexes, and insecurities.

TRANSFORMATION

Dialogic learning transforms people's relationship to their environment. Paulo Freire says,[25] "We are transformative beings and not beings for accommodation." The changes taking place within the field of education are obvious. Nevertheless, various theoreticians and pressure groups have tried hard to convince professionals and groups working towards achieving these transformations that their efforts are useless. The reproduction model proclaimed that education reproduced social inequalities and that nothing could be done about it. Its creator (Althusser) later recognized the frivolity of such arguments,[26] and his followers began to disassociate themselves from them. Bowles and Gintis[27] abandoned their basic thesis. Similarly, Bourdieu,[28] who had also followed Althusser and defended the reproductionist model, said that he had written on the topic in his most structuralist moment, as he now sustains a constructivist structuralism. The most meaningful sociology of education of the following generation was no longer reproductionist: consider the works of Apple,[29] Bernstein,[30] Giroux,[31] Macedo,[32] and Willis.[33] No serious study of the consequences of schooling today can fail to take into account what it transforms, which is just as important as what it reproduces.

Reproductionist theory was conservative and ascientific. It was conservative because it held that while egalitarian educational transformations might be desirable, they were not possible; therefore, it vindicated those who did nothing to help bring about change and attacked those, like Freire, who made the effort to achieve it. It was ascientific because it was based on concepts like Althusserian Marxism, a concept that was elaborated without the reading of Marx.

The poor quality of Althusser's study and the incorrect theoretical and statistical grounding of his followers are now recognized. Unfortunately, however, the reproductionists had for years appeared as if they were clairvoyant intellectuals, exposing what they called the naïveté and lack of scientific basis of emancipatory proposals like Freire's. But with the evolution of the social sciences credence has now been given to transformative alternatives and both the reproduction model and the structuralism it was based upon have been discredited.

Social theories have now proved the dual character of action: system and lifeworld in Habermas,[34] human agency and structure in Giddens;[35] the systemic and structuralist conceptions are challenged, as they considered only one of the two dimensions of action (systems–structures). If society and education are simply consequences of the structures, then people and movements cannot do anything. If intersubjective relationships between people (lifeworld–human agency) generate society and education, then political and pedagogical actions must question what orientation they want to give to the transformations they inevitably produce.

Perspectives on traditional modernity, postmodernity, and dialogicity follow very different approaches on this subject. In the traditional approach, finality is defined by someone who gives him- or herself the role of subject and considers others to be objects to be transformed. In the postmodern, the desirability and even the possibility of transformation are denied.[36] In the dialogical, the possibility and desirability of egalitarian transformations are defended, provided that they result from dialogue and not from the imposition of one person's ideas on the rest.

Within this third perspective, some authors distinguish between social movements fighting for resource distribution (trade unionist) and those fighting for changing the grammar of everyday life (feminist, ecological). I feel it is more useful, for purposes of clarity, to distinguish between corporate-based and solidarist movements. Corporate-based movements lobby for the redistribution of resources or for a directional change favoring certain sectors of society, while excluding the most needy. Solidarists fight for resource distribution and for changes of meaning that benefit all members of society, prioritizing the most needy.

Workers' movements dealing only with the employed, while excluding immigrants and the unemployed, are considered corporative, but so are ecological movements that advocate nature conservation in ways that do not take into account the subsistence requirements of the most underprivileged members of society. Equal rights movements with no sexist, racist, or ageist discrimination are solidarist, but so are syndicalist movements that fight for better working conditions for all workers, transforming relations between employers, wage-earners, unemployed people, and immigrants; these alternatives link equal distribution of resources with a reexamination of the meaning of life. By getting to the root of the problem it is possible to effect change, but trying just to change one symptom results in what the literary group calls "sewing a patch onto ripped pants."

Chelo's participation in the group discussions reflects important personal and social achievements that day by day refute the routine model of reproduction. Laia is also in favor of the transformation that structuralism denies. At first, as a teacher, she wanted to direct Chelo's change, and Chelo in turn wanted to address herself on her own. Reaching agreements and putting aside their differences, they have finally decided that no one directs anyone, that their intersubjective communication orients them both.

Chelo and Laia's communication generates a much more radical and profound feminism than the feminism that had previously been maintained by the teacher and her friends. At first, Laia and her friends believed themselves to be spokeswomen for the ideas on where women's transformations should be headed. The crisis in that conception of traditional modernity generated very different types of reactions in the educators who upheld that conception, depending on whether or not they were encouraging dialogical learning.

The egalitarian dialogue Laia participates in brings about important transformational effects. By removing indifference towards people like Chelo, she redirects attention from the collapse of old transformational perspectives to the search for new ones. The liberating options are now not imposed by some people on others, but created together through horizontal communication among all women. After their disagreements over *Tristana*, the commentary on Sappho's work unites the women in two different stances toward one common liberation.

Some of Laia's friends do not share this attitude. Once their traditional transformative options disappeared, they focused on defending their own corporative and individual interests. They claimed there was no longer any emancipation to be realized. Instead, they wanted to jettison their old liberation ideas in order to do what they had previously criticized as "exploiting the maid" or to be able to date chauvinistic men who kept "their wives" locked up at home. Although they had once chanted "Contra la violación, castración" ("Castration prevents rape"), they later made excuses for a high school teacher who raped a student, and for following Foucault, who advocates the depenalization of rape.

The new emancipatory proposals generate solidarity-based movements that include elements Habermas calls "resource distribution" and others he calls "changes in the grammar of everyday life." The combined activities of the La Verneda–Sant Martí center and of the neighborhood organization coordinator generate redistribution of resources towards the unprivileged. They are not fighting for raises (although they support the solidarist, syndical wage claims), but for free services that indirectly increase the incomes of everyone in the neighborhood. These services are totally nondiscriminatory and thereby benefit everyone, regardless of class, gender, race, age, employment (or lack thereof), or legal residency (or lack thereof).

These actions do not constitute a simple quantitative extension of the same services to new social sectors, but a real qualitative transformation of the means of benefiting from them. The people who participate in the literary circle transform the meaning of their lives in the way they want to. The texts read, comments shared, and educational exclusions overcome lead to the opening up of previously unexplored spaces and experiences. Progressing from a position of exclusion to one of cultural creation profoundly affects their family, work, and personal relationships.

Naturally, this is of no value to reproductionist authors who are officials in the educational system, who do not collaborate with the social sectors attending the gathering or care about the possibility of overcoming exclusion. Their view is that unless everything changes, nothing can change. Since they do not see the possibility for real transformation they just promote themselves intensely, based on their claim that improvement for others is not possible.

INSTRUMENTAL DIMENSION

Protagonists of both conservative and progressive alternatives frequently defend the opposition between instrumental and dialogic learning. Those adhering to traditional positions condemn the excessive use of dialogue in the classroom and the democratization of schools as factors influencing the decline of technical and scientific learning.[37] At the same time, followers of some movements of pedagogical innovation posit humanistic training as counter to technical training. Educators who accept ageist concepts side with this position, as they hold that in adulthood, the individual's capacity for instrumental learning has already decreased. Some writers have even managed to see communicative and instrumental learning in opposition to each other, as the result of a total misunderstanding of Habermas's theory.

Dialogical learning embraces every aspect of learning. It therefore involves the acquisition of all instrumental knowledge and all necessary skills. Dialogic learning is not opposed to instrumental learning, but to the technocratic colonization of learning. That is, it eschews procedures and ends that are not decided by the people, but that are decided by a minority, protecting itself behind technical arguments that obscure its exclusionary interests.

Instrumental learning becomes more intense and profound when situated in an adequate dialogical framework. The ability to select and process information is the cognitive tool that best enables one to function confidently in today's society. Dialogue and reflection encourage the development of that ability. Relationships with other people put not only diverse information but also its selection and processing at our disposal; dialogue helps us choose the most convenient means of public transportation to get to a new job and to use the new computer in the office. Reflection is vital in order to understand fully the tasks we need to accomplish and to use our creativity in finding new solutions to the problems that arise. When dialogue is egalitarian, it encourages intense reflection,[38] since people need to understand other positions and express their own.

Rocío wants to increase her instrumental knowledge and she does it by taking a dialogic position. She rejected the activities of the Francoist Women's Section[39] because people spoke without learning. But she also shunned private learning centers that disregarded the communicative dimension. She wanted to learn while she chatted and to chat while she learned. She has been able to become deeply involved in books like Joyce's *Ulysses*, motivated by the oral commentaries on the readings. She has also overcome the ageism that had her believing at fourteen that it was already too late for her to acquire some basic learning skills.

In the circle people talk while learning literature. There is no syllabus, no curriculum, and no teacher. The next month's topic is not decided in advance. Superficial traditionalists view this approach as entertainment rather than quality instruction. In their conversations, however, people learn more "traditional" content than they do in traditional classes. Many people tackle and assimilate the most important trends, works, and styles in world literature; the historical events and philosophies tied to them; and their relationship to the evolution of other arts.

The fact that the coordinator does not follow a technocratic schedule does not mean that the participants do not plan such a schedule during the dialogical process. The center Lucía's mother went to had traditional classes (dressed up in progressive language) that did not help her acquire instrumental learning. With a dialogical focus, she would have learned more. An obsession with efficiency, when detached from the other aspects that make up human communication, tends to produce inefficiency.

Superficial new-school thinkers find that the literary gathering masks instrumental learning, which is in turn imposed on dialogue; they say that, in fact, people end up deciding to read and to acquire the same type of knowledge that is imposed by traditional teachers. Actually, in dialogical learning, people decide collectively, through discussion, the aims and contents of their discussion. Logically, they include the fundamentals, of which *Crime and Punishment* or *La Regenta* form a part. Neither conservatives nor new-school thinkers encourage the reading of, egalitarian comments on, and personal interpretations of this type of literature.

MEANING CREATION

Dialogic learning is one of the best ways to overcome the loss of meaning that Weber[40] diagnosed in our societies. The replacement of communities by systems is the principal reason for this dramatic absence. In industrial society, bureaucratic systems colonized the social, political, spiritual, and work worlds. In information societies, information systems attempt to control every aspect of our being, including the most personal. Money and power control this offensive, which threatens to convert life into just another product of technical evolution. Groups of people who emigrate from rural villages to big cities suffer that change at an accelerated rate.

Humanity will in the future confront the challenge of recreating the meaning of existence in a universe that is increasingly informational. The energies and referents for that process are found in human beings themselves, in their relationships, in the dreams and feelings they constantly generate.

We can all dream and feel, giving meaning to our lives. The contributions of each person are different and, therefore, irretrievable if not taken into account. Each excluded individual is an irreplaceable loss for the rest. Egalitarian dialogue between men and women provides a place where we can recover that meaning and help direct new social changes in a positive way.

The key factor enabling teaching to make a positive contribution towards that goal is the promotion of equal communication between people. Then, solidarity opens the way towards overcoming the obstacles thrown up by money and power. One way to achieve this is to establish educational settings as spaces for conversing rather than spaces for quiet, passive listening.

Meaning is recreated when interpersonal interaction is actually directed by ourselves. Dialogical learning is based on this principle, which confronts the antihumanist reductionism supporting the systemic colonization of everyday life that we now face. One instance of this reductionism that stands out is the claim that the medium is the message. Dialogic learning affirms, on the other hand, that people create the media, the messages, and the meanings of the messages in our lives. In this way, dialogic learning overcomes the poststructuralist dogma that leads to negation of the human production of the media.

People and their interactions have created speech. They have taken the step from animal gestures to human symbols[41] and to speech.[42] Bureaucratic and information systems, like professional corporations, develop exclusionary linguistic strategies, aimed at maintaining their power over communities. These very strategies, nevertheless, are also created and maintained by people.

The literary circle is a good space for conversation and an excellent means of creating meaning. Kafka's reflection on lack of communication becomes a focal point generating much profound communication. Participants use Kafka's narrative as a way of reflecting and commenting on their own experiences of a systemic destruction of community environments. Their criticism, however, does not lead them to wish for the isolation of the author. On the contrary, it leads them to search for new ways to bond, to replace and improve upon those that have been lost.

The everyday lives of the participants are contained in the colloquia, and vice versa. The styles of conversation found in cafeterias (or *"granjas"*), markets, homes, and factories are all included in the interaction. In an inverse process, what is learned in the sessions is transferred back to those other settings, too. There is no opposition between pedagogical dialogue and everyday speech; rather, there is mutual enrichment and collaboration. Just as the "granjas" revolution incites gatherings, the literary gathering fosters the "granjas" revolution.[43]

Goyo found meaning in literature in a plaza, a mule cart, and a grocery store, all of which served as places to converse with people like Nati. In academic courses structured as places where he had to be quiet, he gained only knowledge that he will never use, as he has no plans to appear on a game show or to show off at an intellectual dinner party.

The continuous experience of sharing ideas with the group helps to recreate the overall meaning of the participants' lives. The difference between the doctor and teacher and the health system and education system exemplifies the change from a personal village organization to the bureaucratic structures of the city that have increasing weight in their lives. The group conversations bring back communal gatherings, projecting them into the participants' present and future in an information society where intense human contact is increasingly necessary.

Juan converts his own reflection and his reflection on the others' reflections into a continual creation of his past, present, and future. His contributions encourage the same process in others as well. Works such as Kafka's would have very limited influence if there were no group intellectuals, like Juan, who recreate the meaning of texts in everyday situations.

The transformative action of this organic intellectual is the inverse of that performed by writers like Althusser. This structuralist author wrote and spoke to maintain his power over those in inferior positions in official hierarchies of knowledge. Juan, on the other hand, creates new life with other people with whom he maintains a horizontal relationship.

SOLIDARITY

The literary circle was formed at the worst time for solidarity-based movements. In the first phase of the information society, social duality imposed the selection of the "best" and exclusion of the rest. Intellectual environments were inundated with fashionable theories proclaiming the futility or even undesirability of efforts at solidarity. This antihumanist trend created a favorable climate for diverse anti-egalitarian reactions: technocratic options, neoliberal politics, and even neo-Nazi movements.

The decline of structuralism and its conservative model of reproduction gave way to a neo-Nietzscheanism that took various forms.[44] The reproduction model had been conservative and ascientific. This new Nietzscheanism (sometimes called poststructuralism) was reactionary and antiscientific. It was reactionary because it considered egalitarian transformations not only impossible, but basically undesirable. The fundamental aim of its proponents was to deconstruct[45] (destroy) all theories or dialogical practices, attempting to demonstrate that they were only generated by power. According to this conception, democracy, equality, peace, or sexual freedom were no better than dictatorship, inequality, war, or rape. The trend was antiscientific because it was against science as a form of knowledge, proclaiming that there was no truth beyond that established by power.

Resisting this antidemocratic current, theories began to arise in defense of solidaristic practices and against those determined by power. Habermas[46] wrote a book rebutting the Nietzschean ideas. Freire[47] noted that one of the most important tasks for progressive intellectuals is to demystify the postmodern discourses with respect to the inexorability of this situation.

Egalitarian educational practices must be grounded in conceptions of solidarity. Habermas's communicative action theory, Freire's emancipatory perspective, CREA's dialogical learning proposal, and many other theories and practices resoundingly affirm that democracy, equality, peace, and sexual freedom are more desirable than dictatorship, inequality, war, and rape, and that education must work in favor of the former and against the latter.

The postmodern trend was superficial,[48] and many of its adherents spoke and wrote about things they had never actually read. Thus, they sometimes tried to base dialogical or egalitarian practices on antidialogical and anti-egalitarian authors like Foucault.[49] This was as unprofessional as trying to ground psychoanalysis on Skinner and behaviorism on Freud. Interesting contributions can be made using any authors (including Nazis such as Heidegger),[50] but by giving their works a new orientation, contrary to the original; also a democratic theorist might use reflections on the army taken from Hitler, but without supporting either him or his ideas. However, in order to foster solidarity you cannot hide behind eclecticism but must be willing to radically reject antisolidaristic theories and practices. No one is neutral; this applies particularly to those who claim to be. As Freire says,[51] "it is not possible to be for someone without being against someone, who is against the one I am for."

Rosalía had directly experienced the exclusionary dynamics promoted by those considered to be at a higher level; this was clear, for example, when she dared to ask, "Who is Marx?" Everything is different at the group meetings, where the collective itself constitutes an environment of solidarity. The literary circle is open to all types of people, and no barriers deter those with little money or no school diploma from joining. The participation of people with little academic training is prioritized. The main motivation behind this action is that everyone learns together, without any "truth" being imposed on the group. Rosalía therefore develops some positions that go beyond exclusionary dynamics, positions that later extend to other settings. Such an attitude leads the group to discuss Joyce's *Ulysses* in spite of the fact that the coordinator originally thought the group incapable of reading it.

Community is another space for solidarity. The gatherings are one activity of the adult education center, solidly integrated into the neighborhood. As part of a coordinating committee, the group participates in the struggles to improve the lives of everyone. When one group of teachers wanted to authoritatively impose a schedule that made it impossible for many people to participate, out of solidarity Rosalía joined in the action against the exclusivist proposal and the relativist and postmodern ideas that legitimated it (ideas such as, "There is no good or bad, all positions have advantages and disadvantages," and even the racist statement, "Things are not all black or white.").

The group also looks at the international aspect of solidarity, especially in relation to peoples facing dramatic problems of war or hunger. The collective reflection resulting from egalitarian dialogue encourages mature and critical stances. People reflect on movements and organizations that, for example, take advantage of solidarity rather than expressing it, organizations whose staff spend on their own travels much of the money that has been contributed, or impose projects on villages that have not asked for them or have even refused them.

Solidarist practices immediately contest the exclusionary research on adult participation in education. Rosalía is all too familiar with the behavior of those who consider themselves to be at a higher level and try to keep others out of their activities. She is quick to put in its place the research that labels unprivileged sectors of society and southern countries as non-participatory. Her experience in living these situations of exclusion, and in overcoming them, contributes to dialogic research ideas that would never have been considered by those with no direct experience of such situations. Rosalía and the other members of the group show their solidarity, worrying mainly about those who do not enjoy the opportunities to participate. Their voices are key contributions that open new possibilities for everyone.

EQUALITY OF DIFFERENCES

Reforms aiming for diversity have created educational inequalities. To overcome them, teaching needs to be reoriented in two ways: the aim of diversity should be changed to that of *equality of differences*, and the outdated conception of meaningful learning should be exchanged for that of dialogic learning.

Equality is the basic value that should orient all progressive education. "Alternative" proposals and reforms have aimed for this; for example, those promoted by African American groups[52] and Gypsy associations.[53] The fight against such movements takes two forms: it either claims the goal is not desirable or maintains that achieving it is impossible.

These conservative reactions are introduced into critical settings by citing alleged limits to or falsehoods in many egalitarian dialogues, but not in order to defend more consistent forms of equality; rather, they abandon this objective and substitute others such as difference, diversity, adaptation, or choice. Difference conceived of as separate from equality generates inequalities. Such an idea supports others that advocate the elimination of checks on the increasing educational differences found in diverse social groups.

Two positions are used in the conservatives' attack: the homogenization of equality and the reduction of "equality"to "equal opportunity." The first argues for the integration of all students into a homogeneous curriculum, which leads to failure on the part of those whose families or communities have different cultures from the one imposed in school. The second aims to give each child the same opportunities to reach high (or low) positions in society, without questioning the inequality between those positions.

Transformative education is based on much deeper and more sincere discourses. Dialogic learning is oriented towards equality of differences, affirming that true equality includes the very right to live in a different way. This perspective, which Freire calls "unity in diversity,"[54] never criticizes limited forms of equality without defending others of more consequence. It never defends diversity without simultaneously proposing equality and fairness toward different people and groups.

Dialogic learning both includes and moves beyond meaningful learning, bringing in factors that help overcome educational inequalities. Often, homogenizing equality is related to objectivism, diversity without equality to an obsolete conception of constructivism, and equality of differences to a dialogical perspective.

In objectivism, a table is a table, regardless of whether or not people use it; reality exists independent of human beings. Basing himself on the works of Weber and Husserl, Schütz[55] developed a constructivist idea affirming that social reality is a human construction dependent on the meaning we give to our actions:[56] the table is a table because we see it as appropriate for activities like writing, playing cards, or having dinner. Freire and Habermas, among others, have developed a communicative concept that includes and goes beyond Schütz's constructivism, pointing out that the meanings we give to our actions depend on the totality of our interactions with other people.

In an objectivist approach, the importance of content is not seen in relation to the students. The teacher's responsibilities are to know the course contents and have the methodological ability to teach them (hence we hear "he knows a lot but he can't teach"). Different students reach different levels of understanding that, sometimes, are countered by new resources for underprivileged groups.

In a constructivist approach, the most important element is the student's learning, not the teacher's teaching. From a single explanation, each student takes a different meaning. Teaching abilities should include research into different processes of meaning formation and the interventions that can improve them.

The dialogical conception includes and goes beyond the constructivist conception, emphasizing one additional crucial factor: the meaning formation process does not depend solely on the intervention of education professionals, but also on all the people and contexts related to the student's learning.

Constructivism's limitations led to one mistake with important social consequences: Constructivist interpretations of Vygotsky's work were used to support some authors' adaptive theories, rather than to remain faithful to Vygotsky's true transformative egalitarian intentions.[57] Among others, the Bielorussian psychologist defended two principles: first, that cognitive development is linked to sociocultural environment; and second, that to improve learning, this environment must be transformed. Though the first principle has been maintained, the problem arises when the second is turned into its antithesis. Instead of transforming context to achieve better learning, adapting the curriculum to the context is proposed.

The obsolete conception of meaningful learning tends to be based on the alleged Vygotsky. In underprivileged areas, adapting curricula to an environment that is not transformed simply reinforces the existing educational inequalities.

Dialogic learning is in tune with Vygotsky's original intent. This perspective leads to the transformation of education centers into learning communities where all the people and groups involved enter into relationships with each other. In this way, the environment is transformed, creating new cognitive development and greater social and educational equality.

Confusion arose during a period of great inequality and relativism that deauthorized the fight for equality. The exaltation of difference was based on several distortions: identifying equality with homogenization, as if there were no people who defended equality by including within it the right to difference; labeling difference as new and equality as old, ignoring the fact that Gypsies and Native Americans have always been considered different and that what is really new is the aim of equality without racist, sexist, or ageist discrimination; and attributing a rejection of universalism to other communities, thereby silencing the excluded voices that demand equal rights.

The alternative to ethnocentrism is not a relativism that still carries with it a great deal of inequality and violence and is a product of white, European, male culture. The solution that excluded cultures are demanding can be found in a dialogical perspective oriented towards exercising the right to egalitarian education; a perspective that, therefore, must take our differences into fair consideration.

Everyone in the literary circle is equal and different. There is not just formal equality, but also, for instance, an equal right to speech. Measures to ensure that the desired fairness becomes more and more of a reality are constantly developed. Participants thereby avoid, for example, a situation in which one person participates ten or more times and another gets no chance to speak.

The group agreed on measures to overcome difficulties as they arose. During one period there was an unequal frequency of contributions, with some people monopolizing the discussion and others not speaking at all. The members decided that each participant should choose a passage from the current book and read it aloud, to introduce her or his own commentary. It was also proposed that another person (usually Goyo or Núria) should act as moderator.

Each participant is different from the others, does his or her own readings, and comes up with his or her own interpretations. The aim of reaching homogeneous opinions or assessments is explicitly rejected. On the contrary, the idea is to develop and maintain personal views on the world and on literature. Dialogue promotes, instead of negating, each person's reflection. Juan does not try to be like Antonio, nor does he try to make Antonio be like him.

Equality is the aim, and this includes an equal right to differences. The right of all individual members to learn what they need and want to learn is defended. This principle of egalitarian dialogue implies a rejection of both ethnocentrism—which does not respect difference—and of relativism—which withholds fairness.

This *equality of differences* is not assured of continuity in other contexts. Outside the group, members occupy different positions based on characteristics such as job, gender, ethnicity, or age. All of them, however, were members of nonprivileged groups before participating in the literary circle, and they continue to be so afterwards. However, their inequality as compared to other groups decreases and in some aspects even disappears altogether. It decreases, for instance, when the cognitive advances a person has made help her or him get a new job or access new resources; it disappears when all of the participants are able to enjoy new activities and have a voice in areas where previously they were silenced.

Antonio finds himself boosted by his participation in the group, as much in his personal and family lives as in his contribution to the community. However, this important step is only one of many that must be taken on the road to a society where nobody suffers from discrimination. Antonio, faced with this fact, chooses to take one small collective step rather than many individual ones. He will not leave his people in the same or worse situation. This Gypsy person is a universal example of solidarity.

NOTES

1. T. W. Adorno et al., *Positivist Dispute in German Sociology* (London: Heinemann, 1976; originally published 1969).

2. J. Habermas, *The Theory of Communicative Action*, vol. 1, *Reason and the Rationalization of Society*; vol. 2, *Lifeworld and System: A Critique of Functionalist Reason* (Boston: Beacon Press, 1984–87; originally published 1981); J. Habermas, *Between Facts and Norms* (Cambridge and Oxford: Polity Press and Basil Blackwell, 1996; originally published 1992).

3. P. Freire, *Pedagogy of the Heart* (New York: Continuum, 1997; originally published 1995).

4. U. Beck, A. Giddens, and S. Lash, *Reflexive Modernization: Politics, Tradition, and Aesthetics in the Modern Social Order* (Cambridge, England: Polity Press, 1994); A. Giddens, *Modernity and Self-Identity: Self and Society in the Late Modern Age* (Cambridge and Oxford: Polity Press and Basil Blackwell, 1991).

5. M. Castells, R. Flecha, P. Freire, H. Giroux, D. Macedo, and P. Willis, *Critical Education in the New Information* Age (Lanham, Md.: Rowman & Littlefield, 1999; originally published 1994).).

6. L. S. Vygotsky, *Thought and Language* (Cambridge: MIT Press, 1986; originally published 1934).

7. J. Habermas, "Multiculturalism: Does Culture Matter in Politics?" (lecture given at the Universitat de Barcelona, 9 April 1997.)

8. E. Durkheim, *The Division of Labor in Society* (Glencoe, Ill.: Free Press, 1947; originally published 1902). In later works his conception bears more similarity to the communicative perspective; among these, see the prologue to the second edition of the above-mentioned book; and E. Durkheim, *The Elementary Forms of Religious Life* (London: George Allen & Unwin, 1965; originally published 1893).

9. T. Parsons, *Toward a General Theory of Action* (Cambridge: Harvard University Press, 1951).

10. E. Goffman, *The Presentation of Self in Everyday Life* (New York: Anchor Press Doubleday, 1959).

11. G. H. Mead, *Mind, Self, and Society: From the Standpoint of Social Behaviorist* (Chicago: University of Chicago Press; 1940; originally published 1934).

12. H. Garfinkel, *Studies in Ethnomethodology* (Englewood Cliffs, N.J.: Prentice Hall, 1967).

13. L. Wittgenstein, *Philosophical Investigations* (Oxford: Blackwell, 1984; originally published 1953).

14. J. L. Austin, *How to Do Things with Words* (Cambridge: Harvard University Press, 1962, lectures given in 1955).

15. H. G. Gadamer, *Truth and Method.* (New York: Continuum, 1975; originally published 1927).

16. R. B. Cattel, *The Discovery of Fluid and Crystallized General Intelligence Abilities: Their Structure, Growth, and Action* (Boston: Houghton Mifflin, 1971), 74–102.

17. R. J. Sternberg and R. K. Wagner, *Practical Intelligence* (Cambridge: Cambridge University Press, 1986).

18. CREA, *Habilidades Communicativas y Desarrollo Social* [Communicative Abilities and Social Development] (Barcelona: Paidos, in press).

19. D. Wechsler, *The Measurement and Appraisal of Adult Intelligence* (Baltimore: Williams & Wilkins, 1958).

20. K. W. Schaie, *Longitudinal Studies of Adult Psychological Development* (New York and London: Guildford Press, 1983).

21. Ageism is discrimination against certain people or groups because of their age.

22. J. Piaget, *The Psychology of Intelligence* (Totowa, N.J.: Littlefield, Adam, 1981).

23. Vygotsky, *Thought and Language.*

24. S. Scribner, *Head and Hand: An Action Approach to Thinking* (New York: Teachers College, Columbia University, National Center on Education and Employment, 1988; ERIC Document Reproduction Service No. CE 049 897).

25. Freire, *Pedagogy of the Heart.*

26. L. Althusser, *The Future Lasts Forever: A Memoir* (New York: New Press, 1995; original work published in 1992).

27. S. Bowles and H. Gintis, "Schooling in Capitalist America: Reply to Our Critics," in M. Cole, *Bowles and Gintis Revisited* (Philadelphia: Falmer Press, Taylor Francis, 1988), 235–45.

28. P. Bourdieu, *Choses dites: Le sens commun* (Paris: Les Éditions de Minuit, 1987).

29. M. W. Apple, *Education and Power* (London and Boston: Routledge & Kegan Paul, 1982).

30. B. Bernstein, *Class, Codes, and Control,* vol. 3, *Towards a Theory of Educational Transmissions* (London: Routledge & Kegan Paul, 1975).

31. H. A. Giroux, *Disturbing Pleasures: Learning Popular Culture* (New York: Routledge, 1994).

32. D. Macedo, *Literacies of Power: What Americans Are Not Allowed to Know* (Boulder, Colo.: Westview Press, 1994).

33. P. Willis, *Common Culture: Symbolic Work at Play in the Everyday Cultures of the Young* (Boulder, Colo.: Westview Press, 1990).

34. Habermas, *Theory of Communicative Action,* vol. 2, *Lifeworld and System.*

35. A. Giddens, *The Constitution of Society: Outline of the Theory of Structuration.* (Cambridge, England: Polity Press, 1985).

36. H. Giroux and R. Flecha, *Igualdad educativa y diferencia cultural* (Barcelona: Roure, 1992).

37. A. Bloom, *The Closing of the American Mind: How Higher Education Has Failed Democracy and Impoverished the Souls of Today's Students* (New York: Simon & Schuster, 1987).

38. Beck, Giddens, and Lash, *Reflexive Modernization*; Giddens, *Modernity and Self-Identity.*

39. General Francisco Franco was dictator in Spain from 1939 to 1975.

40. M. Weber, *The Protestant Ethic and the Spirit of Capitalism* (Englewood Cliffs, N.J.: Prentice Hall, 1980; originally published 1904–5); M. Weber, *Economy and Society: An Outline of Interpretive Sociology* (Berkeley: University of California Press, 1978; originally published 1922).

41. Mead, *Mind, Self, and Society.*

42. Habermas, *Theory of Communicative Action.*

43. Translator's note: "Granja" is the usual term in Catalonia to designate a cafeteria. "Granjas" have become very popular over recent decades, particularly among working-class women, who used to stay at home.

44. The most influential versions were deconstructionism (Derrida, 1967), genealogy (Foucault, 1968), and postmodernism (Lyotard, 1979). The foundations of these currents, however, were the works of Nietzsche (1887) and his Nazi follower, Heidegger (1927). For further information about Heidegger and the Nazi implications of his work and life, see V. Farias, *Heidegger and Nazism* (Philadelphia: Temple University Press, 1989).

45. J. Derrida, *De la Grammatologie* (Paris: Les Éditions de Minuit, 1967).

46. J. Habermas, *The Philosophical Discourse of Modernity* (Cambridge: MIT Press, 1987; originally published 1985).

47. Freire, *Pedagogy of the Heart*, 36.

48. J. F. Lyotard, *La condition postmoderne: Rapport sur le savoir* (Paris: Les Éditions de Minuit, 1979).

49. M. Foucault, *Nietzsche, la Généalogie et l'Histoire* (Paris: Presses Universitaires de France, 1968).

50. M. Heidegger, *Being and Time* (New York: Harper & Row, 1962; originally published 1927).

51. P. Freire, "La pràctica educativa," *Temps d'Educació* (University of Barcelona), no. 1 (1989): 296.

52. R. Edmons et al., "Perspectives on Inequality: A Reassessment of the Effect of Family and Schooling in America," *Harvard Educational Review* 43, 1 (February 1973): 76–91.

53. K. Wang, M. T. Díaz, M. Engel, G. Grande, M. L. Martín, and M. Pérez Serrano, *Mujeres gitanas ante el futuro* (Madrid: Presencia Gitana, 1990).

54. Freire, *Pedagogy of the Heart.*

55. A. Schütz, *The Phenomenology of the Social World* (Evanston, Ill.: Northwestern University Press, 1967; originally published 1932).

56. That idea was circulated by students of Schütz such as Berger and Luckmann, in their book *The Social Construction of Reality* (Garden City, N.J.: Doubleday, 1966).

57. L. S. Vygotsky, *Mind in Society: The Development of Higher Psychological Processes* (Cambridge: Harvard University Press, 1978; originally published 1930–34).

1

Manuel

A Life Spent Struggling against Cultural Inequalities

LITERARY INEQUALITIES

Manuel enjoyed himself in the sessions on *Gypsy Ballads*, but he thought García Lorca was a "señorito,"[1] and he therefore had little sympathy for him. Before moving to the city, his father worked on a farm and had to give part of the crop to a master, who insisted on being called "señorito." Compared to the previous situation of servitude, occupying the lowest position in a big industrial city was a liberation for his family.

García Lorca was anything but an aristocrat. But in the eyes of many workers, he had had an easy life, devoted to parties and creative activities, with plenty of free time. Meanwhile, other people suffered a lot and earned very little, harvesting food, building houses, and washing the clothes of those who spent their time writing. Commenting on the poet's vacation in Cadaqués, instead of concentrating on Lorca's relationship with Dalí and his sister, Manuel emphasized how easy it was to write in those conditions. Words like "beach," "manure," "reading," and "writing" had very different meanings for him than they did for Lorca and Dalí.

Manuel's family makes up part of that group of people that made the development of the 1960s a reality, working hard in factories and getting by as best they could in the slums. His father and two older brothers left Andalusía in 1947 and slept on the beaches of Barceloneta until, after a few months, they managed to get a shack. Once they had a roof over their heads, they decided they were in a position to call the mother and the other six children. In order to avoid paying for one ticket, Manuel, who was then eight, hid under the seat of the train for twenty-four hours. His younger brothers did not pay either, sitting on their mother's lap.

Dalí and his friends also slept on the beach, but in an amazing house. The painter entertained artists and other people with similar lifestyles. The poet Paul Elouard came with his wife, Gala. To seduce her, Dalí—among other things—walked along the sand with his clothes covered in manure. Paul returned to France alone. From that point on, Gala was the wife of one of the richest and most famous painters of the century.

For Manuel, manure was no adornment. In his town, he worked taking care of goats. In Barcelona, he got work transporting packages in a mule-drawn cart. That is where his particular form of reading began: he had to act like a literate worker when he was just a child who did not know how to write. Since the recipients of the packages were always the same people, he memorized the shape of the words that made up their addresses.

When he was eleven he attended a night school class for adults, which he paid for with his tips. The teacher tried to correct his Andalusian accent by hitting him with a ruler. Instead of learning to read and write, what he learned was how school disdained common people.

When he discovered the way writers lived, he saw himself remaining as a manual laborer, or even an unemployed person, forever. When he read after a workday, his main preoccupation was eliminating the wall between literature and the working class. The sentiments of any workmate from the factory were as important for him as the most sophisticated insights of members of the elite.

Goyo, the coordinator of the literary circle, has also worked ever since childhood, although as a youth he only worked during spare time and summer vacations. Until he turned twenty, his main responsibility was school. His first academy, on a busy, unpaved street, followed a kind of intensive teaching program that enabled him to enter a Jesuit school, at the age of seven, with academic knowledge similar to that of his classmates, who came from a higher social class. Since he was good at school, doors opened for him that had been closed to his parents. In fact, he saw Lorca's position in Fuente Vaqueros, Cadaqués, or Harlem not as something unattainable, but as a possible opportunity for his future.

His memories of nights spent by the sea would always be linked to playful

times. At the end of every school year when he was at college, he spent a
night on the wild beaches of Sopelana with a group of friends, reciting
poetry around a fire while they burned their class notes and drank strong
wine punch. It was summertime and the next day they were not going to
work, but to sleep in their comfortable homes. He spent amazing nights
under the stars, but never because he could not have a roof over his head,
nor did he ever work in a factory. His initial training came from teachers,
writers, and critics: he ended up feeling very closed in within academic
walls. Perhaps this is what led him to be so moved by the literary experiences of people like Manuel.

TEARING DOWN ANTIDIALOGICAL WALLS

The contrast between rural life and urban society raised cultural barriers
in Manuel's dialogue, which increased with memories like that of his ap-
palling experience in night school. However, during that period of industrial society, he could get work with almost no formal schooling. At thirteen, he got a steady job in a factory, although his official position as
"illiterate" kept him at the lower levels.

He could not read or write, but he had very attractive abilities; he was a
good flamenco singer, told funny jokes, and was a great conversationalist
and an exciting rabble-rouser. Soon, clandestine organizations started
keeping their eyes on him as a potential spontaneous leader. He had
greater influence at meetings and strikes than he did in his position at the
factory. In addition, he was chosen formally as representative of the workers on the company committee. His "class consciousness" was effecting a
decisive transformation in his life.

At demonstrations and meetings, Manuel showed more ability than his
literate coworkers. The landscape of the workers' struggle was similar to
the rural environment in some ways; oral skills were more important than
school or workshop. For the first time, Manuel could refuse to learn what
society considered necessary; on the contrary, society had to transform itself to value his popular culture. That change gave him self-confidence and
assurance in his criticism of authority.

In that context he heard talk about artists like Picasso, who took part in
the democratic movement, and writers who had come from humble backgrounds. Manuel identified with Miguel Hernández, the Civil War poet,

who had also experienced a poor rural upbringing and had also been a child goatherd. Far from having a frivolous life, Hernández had fought against the dictatorship in both his life and his poetry.

The anti-Francoist environment was different from the only class Manuel had known. Literature did not come from the teacher's authority or from the syllabus, but from intense human sentiment. It was not to be individually studied, but collectively shared. In that movement Manuel discovered poetry by reciting and singing poems such as *Nanas de la cebolla* (*Onion Lullaby*), written in jail by Miguel Hernández when the poet found out that his wife could afford to eat only bread and onions. It was very moving to see a hard man like Manuel almost unable to contain his tears as he sang: "In hunger's cradle/my child lay/on an onion's blood/he nursed away."

Goyo quickly noted that Manuel's artistic sentiments were much more intense than those in most literary circles attended by intellectuals. In his hands, each work generated new hope, recreated from a perspective he never could have imagined. He read with a poignant feeling of exclusion imposed by literate society. Poems like *Nanas de la cebolla* were not written in a peaceful second home by the sea. The poetry that so impressed the group came forth like a cry of pain from the dramatic situation faced by human beings: that of a family's hunger.

THE FALL OF A PROLETARIAN

Reading *Explosion in a Cathedral,* by Carpentier, was challenging for all the people who were directly or indirectly involved in transformative perspectives. Margarita remembered her first advances in the workers' movement, particularly when seeing Víctor enthusiastically describe to Esteban and Sofía the ideas of the Enlightenment and seeing the two men living in the Paris of the French Revolution. Manuel remembered his first doubts when he commented on Víctor's aligning himself with the Jacobins and taking part in the repression of Robespierre, while Esteban worried greatly about the birth of a bureaucracy greatly different from the utopia he hoped for from the revolutionary process. There was a division of opinion when Víctor became governor of Guadelupe, the Caribbean island, bringing in both the guillotine and the abolition of slavery.

The group was very disappointed to read how Víctor first became an authoritarian revolutionary and then a reactionary dictator, reestablishing slavery. They related to Esteban and Sofía's disillusionment with the application of revolutionary ideas. At the end of the book, they identified with these two characters in the reencounter with their ideals: people's transformative need for each other. They liked the hopeful dialogue at the book's close:

Esteban: Who are you going to fight for?
Sofía: For those that were kicked out onto the streets!
Esteban: What!
Sofía: It's something!
Esteban (a little while later): Wait for me!

While commenting on this novel, Manuel told the moving story of the hopes and disappointments of a proletarian fighter. The dream grew during the 1960s and the early 1970s, the best time for the workers' movements in the last period of industrial society. Even in countries where dictatorships prohibited the legal existence of class unions, such unions still existed, achieved wage increases, and developed solidarist actions. They had a firm hold in big businesses where work and life conditions were relatively homogeneous.

Many leaders felt relatively confident and optimistic. The strength of the working class was also the leaders' strength. The positive aspects made up for and overcame the contradictions. The worst feeling for Manuel was his discovery that academic culture was a prerequisite for belonging to the leadership structure even of alternative movements. His fertile oral knowledge, first disdained by school and business structures, later exalted in assemblies, was once again excluded from the higher levels of workers' organizations.

Some authorities in clandestine meetings were workmates who hardly contributed at all in the assemblies, strikes, and demonstrations. The Víctor of Carpentier's novel brought back painful memories of those Manuel now called "bureaucrats." One of them came up to Manuel saying: "Hold a meeting at lunchtime, a strike must begin today." From then on, he was distrustful and very critical of the authoritarian procedures of organizations. Although, like Sofía, he always kept fighting for the people on the lowest rungs of the social ladder, the seeds of disillusionment had been sown in his spirit.

Manuel called the meeting against his will, it was successful, and there was a strike the very same day. He always regretted that. He knew that his words had provoked a predetermined effect, instead of communicating his own feelings. His language had not been sincere: he had instrumentalized his own workmates.

Manuel had realized long before the reading circle was created that the approaches used by workers' organizations lacked meaning in the new situation. Many factories closed down and unemployment became a great worry. Initially, many leaders considered the crisis to be a temporary evil; then they began to discover that industrial society would never return. Their way of life and their convictions were destroyed, and their hopes and transformational will had to be abandoned or updated.

The political transition from dictatorship to democracy opened up possibilities for occupying positions in the administrations. Many "bureaucrats" suddenly experienced radical changes in their ideals and affiliations, which turned out to be very useful in getting them promoted. Manuel was profoundly disillusioned to see how the same workmates who had applauded him as a hero of the workers' movement betrayed their solidarist ideals. However, like Sofía in *Explosion in a Cathedral*, he kept fighting for the rank and file, though he no longer really knew how to do so.

He attributed the crisis at his company to capitalists' theft and pressured the owners to invest more in its restructuring. That way, he retained his radical worker's consciousness that had been generated in traditional industrial society. He also faced union negotiations.

When the workers decided to keep the factory open, organizing themselves cooperatively, new hope blossomed. Now there would be no capitalists stealing benefits, and the product of the workers' activity would be for the collective. Class-based hierarchies disappeared: giving in to the powerful in order to feed one's family would no longer be necessary. At last, the factory would be a group of free and equal people, with comradeship heading towards solidarity with the working class in general.

Later developments caused Manuel a great deal of suffering but also made him search for new perspectives on his struggle. Worker management led to innumerable difficulties, particularly when some workers took advantage of the absence of hierarchical control to pass the buck on to their workmates. This was not capitalist selfishness or bureaucratic selfishness, but that of the rank and file. It had never seemed so hard to achieve a solidarist transformation of society. On this occasion, dejection reached the deepest of his convictions.

At the end of the 1970s many people experienced the same despondency. The social environment was contaminated by attacks designed to stifle the principles of the emancipatory movements. The aim of equality began to be replaced by the aim of difference. Activism was criticized to the point of being labeled as the worst of all totalitarianisms. Values like relativism and indifference to injustice were proclaimed. The material and spiritual identity of the industrial proletariat fell into total crisis.

PRODUCING SOCIAL EXCLUSION

When the working-class neighborhood where Manuel lived mobilized and acquired an adult education center with the slogan "It's never too late to learn," the gleam in his eyes reappeared. On the one hand, he had to learn new things to adapt to new working conditions. On the other, he thought he had found a new way of carrying on his fight for justice.

From the beginning, he concentrated on social themes. Before mastering reading and writing, he managed through oral communication to expound a global vision of society and explain the dramatic crisis of the industrial working class. He posed questions and polemicized with force until his own reflections clarified his perceptions.

The crisis at the plant was more than the result of capitalist greed or betrayal by some union leaders: it was a global process in which executives, union leaders, and workers experienced tremendous difficulties in restructuring. As ever, a few privileged people reaped the benefit by getting rich while the majority lived in misery. But it was useless for Manuel to express his opposition as he had done before. He had to find new forms of action and, like Sofía, he had to maintain his egalitarian principles even without knowing how to defend them.

The inner strength of Manuel's rebellion was much more intense than the rigidity of his traditional style of fighting. The concept of changing landscapes reawakened his social enthusiasm. The breakdown was not of solidarity in general, but just of its typical manifestations in industrial society. Participating in the clarification of the new situation filled him with hope, as did planning other means of searching for equality.

But who were the underdogs now? It was so clear before on the concept of working class! Along with reacting to the continual decrease in stable employment and the change in the types of stable employment available, many employees were motivated only by personal objectives, ignoring the solidarist or general interest of the overall working population. The weakest people, unemployed or underemployed, were excluded from the corporative movements of the rest.

Speaking with other people, Manuel found explanations for this break in worker solidarity. The informational revolution decreased the availability of work hours in the formal market. This fact could be used to support an egalitarian social model by reducing the workday and distributing the employment equally, and to support an anti-egalitarian model by reducing the number of jobs and increasing unemployment.

In the 1980s, there was a massive offensive. Choosing "the best" to manipulate new technologies led to the exclusion of the rest. The over-forty-fives who had not finished their obligatory schooling were considered non-recyclable for new forms of work and classified as a sector to be excluded.

According to what Manuel had heard one politician say, the same had occurred in the industrial revolution. First, living conditions worsened for many people, like miners, but then important improvements were made, like the eight-hour workday and welfare. Perhaps these concerns led the group to choose a reading from the industrial revolution period.

Germinal was greatly enjoyed. Zola moved the collective with his description of the life and rebellion of the miners and their families. The naturalist author's way of referring to spiritual poverty as well as material misery stood out, with numerous internal conflicts seen even within the working class itself. There was no simplistic vision of good workers and bad capitalists; on the contrary, some people were indignant about Etienne (the strike leader), who showed more concern for his own future than for his dead workmates.

Manuel insists that a new type of poverty is being created today. He rejects the vision of the information society as another step in the progress of humanity. He says that we are on the brink of a poverty that affects his family, friends, neighbors, and coworkers; he also feels that people as a whole have gone through a dramatic spiritual impoverishment.

He affirms that many struggles like those in *Germinal* will be necessary to improve the conditions of all people and not just a select few. The eight-hour workday and social services were not gifts from the capitalists; they were wrenched from them by the force of the workers' struggles. "We cannot trust them to share what they get out of the informational revolution, nor should we expect them to want to. Now also we must fight to escape our poverty."

Sensitivity to inequality was and always will be fundamental to Manuel's commentaries. After having read this book, *Sharing Words*, he wrote:

> In this hard and troubled life, "Lazarillos"[2] from innumerable families in the country and in capital cities run all over the planet, with no clothes or food, while at the same time tons of blind people cover their eyes in order not to see the poverty. . . . Hearing about Goyo's times on the beach at night by a fire, I felt the desire of my youth to have had friends, to be able to go to the beach in the moonlight with naked bodies and guitars and castanets, singing to the night the same way that long ago cavemen sang to the earth till the sun came up.

RETURN OF THE EMANCIPATORY SPARK

In the movement in support of the adult education center, Manuel and his words regained relevance in the group. The others, far from being a homogeneous group, were made up of diverse types, including industrial workers, unemployed people, homeworkers, elderly people, and young people. This sense of popular community evoked sweet memories of Manuel's childhood in a small town.

In those community assemblies and meetings, all the people could express their own ideas and feelings, with no outside authority telling the spontaneous leaders what they should propose. The people acted according to their own interpretations of their problems, instead of having bureaucrats' ideas imposed on them.

The participants in the adult education center movement felt they were the protagonists of their own movement and, increasingly, of their own lives. The people in the neighborhood dreamed about the type of neighborhood they wanted, organized their idea in a plan and fought for it, and at the same time negotiated with representatives of the administration and of private enterprises. They decided collectively when to change an aim and when to engage in a show of strength. More general citizens' initiatives against racism, sexism, and other inequalities were also incorporated in their plan. The people were not objects of leaders and organizations, but subjects of their own actions.

Earlier, Manuel had gone through a real crisis, which led to a lack of faith in people. He felt the fall of the industrial model of worker solidarity as if it were that of all solidarist movements. Besides, those who had participated in the strikes now voted for parties that upheld the capitalist strategy. He felt they had surrendered to the system.

Finally, he found a popular organization oriented towards a global transformation of society. The neighborhood association's committee fought for equality and obtained free services to improve the quality of life of all the residents. The diversity of the participants and the objectives proposed facilitated the forging of new relationships between people of different genders, ethnicities, and ages, as well as connections with different cultures and institutions.

At the age of eleven, Manuel had paid tips, equivalent to one-third of his salary, to a teacher who used to hit him with a ruler and give negative assessments of his learning abilities. Attending high-quality classes that were free was equivalent to an indirect raise in pay for everyone.

Manuel's social dream was reborn of the everyday demonstrations of solidarity shown by such different types of people. Though they might vote for parties unfavorable to workers, they were excellent companions, they transformed their lives profoundly, and they even firmly confronted the political groups they had voted for when they thought these groups were acting unjustly. Now Manuel was discovering that people who had previously seemed to him objects of capitalism were creative subjects of new relationships and realities.

The revolutionary perspective was more than a paradise promised for the future; it was something in the air in the present. The emancipatory spark could be seen in people's eyes when they talked about the feelings that their readings had inspired and the transformations, personal and collective, that they were bringing about.

JUMPING FENCES

When he signed up at the adult education center, Manuel had two aims: to learn to write and to get a diploma. Following the course had advantages but also disadvantages. Getting over his illiteracy complex led to a new frustration: the difficulty of eliminating many of his spelling mistakes. He refused to go from literacy class to new readers' class until he had done this.

He even went to another center for a while when in La Verneda they insisted he change to a higher level.

Speaking of his doubts about the literary circle, his question was: "Is this the way to correct my mistakes?" Goyo answered that considering his linguistic diversity as a mistake was a barrier that the elite had set up with regard to the majority's learning, and he proposed that Manuel concentrate on improving his comprehension and self-expression. Manuel's answer made the teacher rethink many things: "Sure! That sounds good, but you wouldn't be a teacher if you made my mistakes, and I won't pass a qualifying exam for a job if I need to as long as I make them."

Goyo understood that it was one thing to get rid of the barriers to learning and quite another to need to jump over these barriers while they still existed. In any case, it was dishonest to deny others a right that you have already exercised, to question the importance for Manuel of eliminating his spelling mistakes when you made none and had thereby gotten a diploma and a job.

Later, the group read and discussed *Hopscotch*. Cortazar's book, considered by many to be the best twentieth-century novel written in Spanish, recreates the life of Argentinians in Paris and their return home. The group was enthusiastic about the author's rebellion against "order" seen in his fantastic *Cronopios and famas*; in these short stories, "cronopios" are people who squeeze the toothpaste tube carelessly and "famas" are those who worry about wasting toothpaste.

Hopscotch surprised international critics for different reasons. It can, for example, be read in two ways: by following the traditional order or in another sequence. Chapter 69 is ritin with fonemik spelling. It seems strayng at furst, but much eezeeur than akshual ofishul norms for peepul hu ar lurning to rite and evun eezeeur for peepul hu speek with foneems that difur frum ofishul wuns. Thuh peepul from thuh grup started to rite as thay spok and reeuhlizd that thay no longer mayd mistayks. Silent letuhrs disapeerd, az did tu wayz uv speling thu saym wird. Difrent pronunsiashuns permit difrent spelings. But then, cuhd a brit understand a sutherner, if thay yuzd difrent spelings? Yes, in thu saym wey thay understand eech uhther wen thay speek yuzing difrent foneems.

In the nineteenth century Andrés Bello proposed a phonemic reform of spelling for the Spanish language. If we had listened to this Latin American linguist, the direct correspondence between phonemes and graphemes would have simplified literacy and would have created respect for the diverse uses of language. The reform would have eliminated an important cultural cause for exclusion and would have converted Manuel's errors into linguistic richness; he could have written "sapato" instead of "zapato" without being punished by his first teacher or by the institutions of literate society. In any case, *Hopscotch*'s phonetic chapter made the participants see their difficulties as a social error on the part of those with the power to impose "correct spelling," instead of a personal deficiency of their own.

The group's reaction showed Goyo that he had acted frivolously by defending the Andalusian accent to the extent of minimizing the need to learn established norms of spelling. Attempting to correct his error, he explained that at the meetings it was hard to specifically take on error correction, that there was another class with that aim. But he also suggested that reading and collective discussion could encourage the learning of different things, spelling included. Manuel finally made a decision, took part in the literary group, and reintegrated himself into formal classes, gaining a diploma in spite of some continued problems with spelling.

BETWEEN POPULAR AND POPULISM

At first, Manuel only enjoyed books written by people whose political positions were clearly in favor of the working class and books that, in addition, described working-class lives and struggles. Miguel Hernández died in the prisons of the dictator Franco and his *Nanas de la cebolla* is a dramatic song of the suffering of the people. Zola was involved in the Dreyfus case and died in strange circumstances (his *Germinal* is perhaps the first proletarian novel); Víctor Hugo was in favor of the Paris Commune and *Les Misérables* speaks of rebellion.

It was hard for Manuel to accept some people's enthusiasm for Borges's *Fictions.* This writer took a confused position during the last Argentinian dictatorship and wrote stories about and for intellectuals, disregarding people with popular knowledge. Manuel was angered by people's interest in stories like *Pierre Menard, Author of the Quixote,* in which the novel is recreated by the Cervantes translator, giving importance to the reflection of the Argentinian writer's own experience: Borges read the English version of the Quixote before reading Cervantes' Castilian original, and thus the original always seemed to him to be an inept translation of the English rather than vice versa. The group discussed the idea of writing's independence from its author, defending different interpretations by each reader.

Some people refused to take part in these assessments, as it seemed to them that experiencing the multiplicity of texts through the translation of a novel was as elitist as the aristocratic parties mentioned earlier. They felt that the high regard for the work was more connected with its exclusivity, which limited its access to a minority, than with its quality. Some of the group reacted with a populism that valued only literature that came out of popularly oriented social realism. The image of Zola, scribbling notes on any small-town street corner where there was life, was considered a fine example of this.

The growing interest in French naturalism and realism led the group to read Balzac and Flaubert. *Papá Goriot* was seen as an incredible insight into the greedy lifestyle generated by capitalism. While Goriot, the father, dies alone, after having dedicated himself totally to the love of his daughters, Rastignac courts one of them and his infinite avarice is revealed. The group was particularly disappointed to find out that such critical writings had been penned by a writer as selfish as Rastignac. They felt genuinely deceived when they learned that Balzac's own aspiration was to become one of the four most important men of the nineteenth century, thereby placing himself on the same level as his hero, Napoleon.

A miserly man wrote a magnificent and exhaustive account of others who were like him. Indeed, perhaps his critique reached such penetrating levels precisely because he described what he knew firsthand. Little by little, the group began to value literature more for the interpretations of those who read it than for the opinions and lives of those who wrote it. They became convinced that the common people would lose out if they excluded certain readings from their list.

The debate generated arguments about the effects of socialist realism. Some members of the group claimed that Stalinism had imposed the subordination of art that bureaucrats considered to be of interest to the proletariat. The bureaucrats, in fact, considered the working class to be intellectually inferior or naive observers. If a painting represented a man working, he had to be sad if he was in a capitalist factory and happy if the factory was socialist. The bourgeoisie were all evil and party leaders all good, except those who were labeled traitors.

The group considers people as subjects of their own interpretations. This perspective is consistent with the story of *Pierre Menard,* rather than with a

writer like Borges, who excused the Argentinian dictatorship. If this translator could recreate a Quixote different from Cervantes', the literary circle's
members could also recreate *Papá Goriot* and any other work without letting
the author's life limit the creation. Dialogue transforms an avaricious
man's novel into a radical criticism of avarice and a heated defense of solidarity.

TEARING DOWN ELITIST WALLS

Authorities erect walls between certain types of literature and certain types
of people. Both literal and metaphysical powers are at work. Stalinism was
a literal power for those who lived in Eastern Europe during the dictatorship and a metaphoric one for groups in other countries who dogmatically
followed Stalin's orders. Unlike literal powers, metaphorical ones can be
dissolved through dialogue.

In the literary circle there were no literal powers, but there were metaphorical ones. The most important was the dominant conception of
"high" culture. Manuel felt this barrier produced negative effects not only
on the population but also on art itself. On the one hand, the majority of
the people were excluded from the study of certain books. On the other,
literature could not be enriched if it was isolated from the interpretations
and readings of common people.

The group's discussions referred to concrete circumstances in the participants' lives. The needs, desires, opinions, and dreams of people like the
group members differ from those found in the elite: they spring forth from
personal and social experiences full of basic problems. Literature brings
new perspectives to their lives, and their lives add unusual interpretations
to literature. Both are thereby mutually enriched and transformed.

Self-confidence grows as walls are torn down. People exercise their own
right to make decisions—with no external impositions—on what is interesting to read, what is valuable, or what is trivial. They do not ask permission
to become second-rate members of reading groups who look at selected
texts. If they did, their interpretations would be seen as deficient, as their
popular knowledge is looked down upon and seen as ignorant by "high"
society.

People like Manuel burst through the restrictive area of classical literature, breaking down elitist barriers. Texts are resources for what Freire has

called "cultural communication," the creation of new knowledge based on people's own identities and on dialogue with other people, including those who wrote the texts.

The readings change people's views of themselves, their families, and their friends. The participants break down some barriers, because the exclusion they suffer under the label "ignorant" is weakened when they see that most people with higher levels of education do not read this type of literature. On the other hand, other problems arise; for example, when they begin taking books into other rooms of the house, instead of spending so much time watching television with other family members.

As always, transformation is ambivalent; it creates interactions with personal and social consequences, with new advantages and disadvantages. All of these repercussions take place in the specific circumstances lived by each participant. The group's practical perspective is the result of the concrete environments in which its members' lives unfold.

Academic and upper-class circles see this practical focus as the result of an artistic deficiency. They despise the people's tastes, while aggrandizing the views of the "selected few" as if they were the only ones to possess a pure aesthetic sense. Dialogical action overcomes these prejudices by demonstrating that the members of the elite also relate readings to their particular contexts. Goyo especially picks up on metaphors because they are relevant in his academic environment. People in the group—like Manuel—think more about how characters in the books or their writers make ends meet, because that is a continual issue of their everyday reality. Both approaches are ways of living art; neither is better or worse than the other, just different.

Inequality in the information society creates unequal readings as well. The danger is that some are excluded as deficient. Common people do not tend to read classics for economic, cultural, and social reasons. Besides, when they do, their interpretations are considered artistically inferior. This is the formula that sets Manuel apart from the debate in which walls are erected between popular knowledge and official knowledge. Cultural dialogue, on the other hand, includes popular participation in the elaboration of knowledge, instead of reducing such participation to the extension to all people of what is classified as superior knowledge.

Manuel felt intensely the lack of attention given to the basic problems—hunger, unemployment, illiteracy—of needy people within the elitist landscape. The few times these problems are taken into consideration, they are viewed from the point of view of people who had never dealt with such needs firsthand. This criticism did not lead him to claim that only miners could write about miners, that only people employed in particular jobs could read and discuss literature about their jobs; he felt that miners, waitresses, and homeworkers could all write or speak about intellectual literature, just as intellectuals write about all sorts of people.

When this egalitarian process is generalized, we will see significant social and artistic improvements. Artistically, literature will be enriched with new dialogues and dimensions. Socially, new perspectives will be created to confront basic problems faced by the population. For Manuel, the basic question is whether literature has anything to do with the lives and cultures of all of humanity or whether, on the contrary, it is just another activity of the elite.

NOTES

1. "Señorito," in Spanish, refers to a master. This word has the connotation of the master giving himself airs.

2. The reference is to *Lazarillo de Tormes*, a picaresque novel describing the life of the destitute child of the title.

2

Lola

From "Illiterate" to Creator of a Literary Circle

ANTIDIALOGICAL BARRIERS: PERSONAL, CULTURAL, AND SOCIAL

Lola had fond memories of Federico García Lorca. They were both from Fuente Vaqueros and met in a San José farmhouse. As a child she loved Federico because he was always willing to play; at the time, no one knew he would become an important writer. Sixty years later, she still laughs when she explains how they played a trick on the mayor.

She was hit hard by the assassination of the man who sang, told stories, played ring-around-the-roses, and gave her piggy back rides so freely. From that moment on her teacher did not dare bring up the poet in class, although she did when they spoke at home. Lola had spent her childhood in a liberal atmosphere and her adolescence was quite hard, in the authoritarian environment that was imposed with the end of the Spanish Civil War. Since her concerns far surpassed the role official teachings reserved for women, she built up a barrier against dialogue in a school where "more than studying, they taught me to embroider."

Forty years later, the transition to democracy permitted the development of progressive adult education centers. Lola returned to her studies as an adult and found the atmosphere there more like the parties at the farmhouse than the authoritarian school she had attended as a child. Instead of hiding the importance of García Lorca or doubting his worth as a human being, participants valued him as a person and a writer. The appreciation of Federico and the liberal atmosphere united her so intimately to the project that she was able to overcome the personal barriers she had erected to keep out educational communication.

She enrolled in a class in functional literacy. The La Verneda–Sant Martí adult education center was founded by a neighborhood movement and was committed to developing the abilities of all the people who attended it. However, in the so-called formal classes, certain academic obligations had to be met and these, at times, made the teaching appear too similar to that at a regular school.

Lola's views of culture still came from the informal gatherings she had observed in her childhood. In classes, though, there were syllabi and evaluations. Although people talked a lot, she could not always let her imagination loose. For Lola, with training that was rich and yet not at all academic, a cultural wall was thrown up, hindering dialogue. When she had to pass through the filter of scholastic dynamics, regardless of how mellow and unbureaucratic they were, Lola felt as if she was up against a wall.

In the literary circle, there was no program to be followed. If people wanted to, they could read and discuss García Lorca for the entire semester; if not, they could move on to another writer after the first session. During these conversations, she was able to savor once again the flavor of her childhood, and her cultural communication barriers were weakened.

Her attitude towards teaching staff changed radically. In the decades after the Spanish Civil War, she had developed a great distaste for priests, doctors, and teachers, three traditional powers that imposed very restrictive norms on the everyday lives of women. In that atmosphere, her husband prevented her from working as a midwife, and it was years before she was allowed to work in a doctor's office. Along with many others, she referred to doctors as "high and mighty." García Lorca, a man of caliber, had treated her as an equal, and yet any "old Joe" with an academic title and official authority could look down his nose at her. Her dialogue with religious, health, and educational institutions was cut off by social barriers.

The situation changed in this new educational project. The teaching team spoke to all the participants as equals. Among the volunteers who taught classes, there were people who had been participants like herself and who used the same language. One collaborator was a doctor who told health jokes in an atmosphere of total equality, where Lola would have expected to find the "high and mighty." Her children made it clear to her that she had every right to study and to go out with friends. Many social walls that had inhibited communication disappeared in an environment where none of the participants considered themselves more cultured than the rest, regardless of whether they were students in the literacy class, doctoral students at Harvard, or university professors.

CULTURAL INTELLIGENCE: OVERCOMING THE BLINDERS OF ACADEMIC CULTURE

Goyo is a teacher and neighborhood activist. At one time he was researching the history of adult education. He loved old libraries, where he passionately read every document he could find about the cultural activities of workers' movements at the turn of the century. Cultural associations and popular universities were true spaces of alternative creativity.

He discovered a reference to a readers' guide for workers, used at the beginning of the twentieth century at the university extension in Asturias for the mining population. It was written by Rafael Altamira and was called *Lecturas para obreros: Indicaciones bibliográficas y consejos*. Goyo expected to find in it simple readings or revised editions of classics, summarized and adapted for the supposedly inferior abilities of the working classes at the turn of the century. He was pleased the day he found that guide, although what he found within it produced great insecurity in him and made his faith in his many years of classroom studies falter. What he read spoke of reading aloud excellent classics such as *The Odyssey* and *The Divine Comedy*.

After reading the text, Goyo lost himself in memories of key relationships in his life. As a child, he had spent some summers in a village with no cars or tractors, just animals and carts that transported people and goods. One morning, everyone ran towards an open space. Young Goyo scrambled through the adults' legs until his eyes lit upon the exciting spectacle: a man was singing passages from a play, while showing a series of pictures that looked like the comics sold in city kiosks. Two or three years later, he was in a donkey cart with a peasant who had no schooling. The man recited Calderón de la Barca with a glint in his eyes that many university professors lack.

The words of the readers' guide, incomprehensible to the mind of a professional academic, were mixed with Goyo's childhood memories, until they returned to him full of meaning. Lola remembered her friend Feder-ico, looking at her new literature teachers who resembled him. The people at La Verneda were highly motivated by literature. They needed no motiva-tion to express themselves; all they needed was no longer to be excluded.

But Goyo did not seem to have the right words or culture to overcome the exclusion. He decided that the best he could do was to communicate through total silence, in place of his habitual pedagogical discourse, by lis-tening to the others' impressions. He took the open space of the trouba-dour and the peasant's donkey cart as the models, rather than the class-rooms he had passed through. He thought that, instead of teaching his own point of view, he would listen to the people's comments. For them to learn, he did not have to teach anything; instead, he would learn along with them. The pedagogy of explaining had to be replaced by the pedagogy of listen-ing; and if such a thing did not exist, it had to be invented.

Acting as an intellectual transformer, he decided to move beyond all the deficit theories he had learned at college and began to search for new types of knowledge. As at other times, before falling back on science, he sought out inspiration and orientation in literature. Many manuals declared that it was difficult to read texts that include metaphors. But García Lorca says that everyone creates metaphors because language is made of images. Peo-ple use the word "wing" to describe the part of a roof that sticks out, "heaven fat" to name a type of candy, a "noodle" is a head, and "pie" is something easy.

Goyo remembered the seminars he had given to anti-Francoist leaders. Working-class people tended to reach out or listen to the writings of Marx or Bakunin with more interest, intuition, and critical perspective than many college students. They had a low academic level, but they looked at the texts very closely, since they deemed them to have great influence on their own lives. Those readings were different from college classes: they spoke of daily debates in factories, clandestine organizations, and homes.

To get the scientific community to accept what were really discoveries from the narratives, he had to probe deeper into the latest research. He found studies proving that human intelligence can keep increasing throughout adulthood, instead of necessarily decreasing after childhood. Other studies made it clear that adult intelligence was different from pre-adult intelligence, which was why people in the group learned differently from children and teenagers in the school system.

This research enabled Goyo to move beyond theories about the decrease in intelligence that underestimate the abilities of adults. The literary circle coordinator quickly tuned in to new studies, thanks to conversations with people whose learning was blocked. Lola had told many stories; she knew lovely songs that García Lorca had collected about popular knowledge. A woman from the literacy class had taught Goyo this one: "The moon is a tiny well/flowers ain't worth nothing/worthy are your arms/when they hug me at night."

When she heard that these ballads were "octosyllabic verses with an alternating assonant rhyme scheme," Lola asked for an explanation and then, without paying much attention, said: "very interesting." The next day Goyo asked her if she knew what octosyllabic verses were, and she answered with a question: "What about you? Do you know how to sing them?" He thus learned that the "ballad" had very different meanings for each of them; his was based on academic intelligence and hers on practical intelligence. But they could both develop their collective cultural intelligence and overcome their respective academic and practical limitations.

The teacher felt awkward and ridiculous singing those verses. He discovered that Lola could teach him a much richer and more poetic approach to ballads than the one he had learned at school. They shared a dialogical process revolving around this composition and around literature in general. Lola told of her warm memories of García Lorca as a person, and Goyo listened in a way he had never been able to do in a classroom.

HABERMAS CONVERSES WITH THE GROUP PARTICIPANTS

Lola was more interested in reading and discussing García Lorca's poems than she was in gaining a diploma. Manuel was obsessed with correcting the spelling errors he blamed on his Andalusian accent. Chelo wanted to share friendship and conversation after the traumatic death of her husband. Rocío was in search of improved reading comprehension in order to continue her basic studies. Juan wanted to read and understand lots of books. Rosalía needed to rid herself of the frustration she felt at being called uncultured. Antonio enjoyed playing the guitar to accompany popular songs. Instead of debating the best option, they all created processes that were open to diversity.

It was agreed that everyone would read the same text, but each person for her or his own reasons. At first they spoke with great insecurity: they thought their contributions would be better if they were similar to those of the teacher, the authors of the encyclopedia, the literary critics, or the author; if the group members' readings were contrary to these others or simply different, they thought they lacked the knowledge needed to grasp the true meaning of the text. Theirs was a profane knowledge, that of people who were not experts on the material. Cultural authorities had sacred knowledge; their interpretations were correct because they were endorsed by powerful figures and those figures' knowledge, regardless of whether or not they were accompanied by convincing arguments.

Lola's anarchistic temperament was of great help in giving each person's interpretations as much value as that of the encyclopedia. She accepted only what she understood; one day she wrote: "What I didn't like about religion was how the priest and the monks made me learn the doctrine, and I didn't understand it so I used to explain it in my own way; then they would punish me and ask me to say it just as it was written, that was why I didn't like people who made me say it just as it was written, they scared me."

Juan believed greatly in "authorized" sources and spent much time reading them. Soon he realized that their interpretations often disagreed and he began to doubt them all. They became references like any others when it came to explaining his own vision, just like the opinions of the rest of the group.

Each time new people joined the collective, the same debate resumed: Was there such a thing as the correct interpretation of a text or were multiple readings possible? People felt trapped within the narrow confines of profane knowledge, unable to tear down the walls dividing them from the sacred knowledge that was made available only to those who had been to college.

They began by feeling unable to create new meanings, only understanding part of the writers' creations and the teacher's interpretations. Sometimes they stared at the pages as if they contained a secret, hidden meaning. The teacher, however, possessed this secret meaning, thanks to a mysterious and foolproof relationship with the author. It was as if they were both in the same club, in the same "scholars' heaven."

Discussing one of García Márquez's anecdotes was very useful in this debate. The daughter of a friend of his took a literature exam in which she had to respond to the question: In the title of *One Hundred Years of Solitude,* why is one of the e's written backwards? The teacher was so sure of the connection between the book title and the literary characteristics that he proclaimed this knowledge and turned it into exam material. In reality, though, the author himself had called the editor to find out who had set the letter backwards and why.

Acting as he did, this teacher put up a sacred wall that acted as a barrier to dialogue, placing truth in an aesthetic sphere that only wise men like García Márquez and the teacher himself had access to. He was the stereotypical antidialogical teacher who feels that discussions are unnecessary and does not search for the truth because it does not exist. He finds only his own reading interesting, because it is creative or simply because it is his. All else resides outside the sphere of brilliance, creativity, or novelty and is confined within the walls of the populist or utopic. From this aristocratic stance, universal communication is impossible and all that is worthwhile is open discussion among a select few. This is an extreme case of a sacred cultural wall that excludes the majority from creative activity.

Lola spoke enthusiastically about this anecdote. The comments were very helpful to her in overcoming sacred walls and feeling secure in the importance of her own commentaries. The group read new texts knowing that all people, even ordinary people, can create new meanings.

Years later, Habermas gave a lecture at the Universitat de Barcelona on the "Intercultural Discourse on Human Rights." Some people from the literary circle attended, joining an almost entirely academic audience. Mariana dared to raise her hand. Goyo became tense, foreseeing the exclusionary reaction she would receive as soon as she began to speak. He quickly prepared a possible intervention, but he soon decided it would be unnecessary. He knew that the speaker would understand Mariana better than any of the pseudointellectuals who might dare to scorn her. He remembered situations he had shared with Habermas in which the author had proven his egalitarian spirit, making a long trip with five people in a compact car or contentedly eating typical student meals.

Mariana asked about women's work rights. She did not do it with the pompous tone and language expected in a classroom. Some professors and students reacted with distaste and even sarcasm. Mariana was not of a standard to be participating in such an activity, they felt. She knew how to respond: "I don't talk like an intellectual but I know what I mean."

Habermas resolved the situation by applying his own proposed universal dialogue. Everyone has the right to set forth his or her line of reasoning, using her or his own tone and language. He began by saying: "That is a brilliant and very critical question." Many people's smiles froze and then faded into expressions of respect or, at least, acceptance of the lesson learned from one who held a higher position than their own.

The speaker went on talking about the importance of planning to achieve human rights in our own societies. He thereby directly addressed the issue faced by the La Verneda center, which was at the time going through an intense debate over a bill of rights for participants in adult education programs. As opposed to some others, Mariana proposed that women be specified, in writing, as belonging to a sector of society suffering especially from discrimination. This is what she had been thinking about in the seconds before she spoke, not about whether she would receive acclaim for speaking out. Her motivations stemmed from her solidarity with a popular movement, not from the desire to keep up appearances in academic circles.

The group was as pleased with Habermas and with one part of the audience as they were displeased with another section. At the time, they had been discussing Joyce's *Ulysses*. They asked themselves how many of the professors and students who had considered them unworthy of participating in the dialogue actually read that kind of book. Mariana went even further when she noted: "One of the professors who protested slept through the entire lecture."

DIALOGIC RATIONALITY: THE POWER OF REASONING VERSUS THE REASONING OF POWER

Calling the group a literary circle conveyed the idea of open conversation rather than that of a teaching program and made it easier to avoid the mechanisms of power typically found in the school system. It recovered the essence of adult education, initiated in the eighteenth century at egalitarian, unclassified gatherings that had no predefined teacher or student roles. Later, official school procedures colonized many of these dialogues.

Many classes worked under the hierarchical principle that who holds power holds reason. Under this view, if students are not clear on something, it is because either they lack the capacity to understand the teacher or the teacher explains poorly. But instead of being constructed by everyone, knowledge already exists and is possessed by the teacher, who then transmits it to the class. The only people with more knowledge are those with more authority, such as authors and theorists.

Those authorities are easier to criticize than to change, and their views are rooted in the participants themselves. Traditional teaching is rejected in the literary circle, yet at the same time, people wish for some of its aspects. At first, it was hard to put reason in the place of power. In fact, the intellectual fashion of the time affirmed that "power creates everything." Many professionals defended their authoritarianism and rejected any democratic and egalitarian transformation of learning.

The La Verneda–Sant Martí center has the clear aim of fighting for cultural equality for the whole population. Rather than basing education on the reasoning of power (that is the way it is because the teacher says so), the center bases education on the power of collectively agreed reasoning: after a dialogue in which everyone contributes freely, people reach agreements such as which book should be read next.

In accordance with this orientation, Goyo acts like any other participant, although the habits of educational power make it impossible for there to be complete equality. When was García Lorca born? Why did the Francoists kill him? Were all the writers of the Generation of '27 followers of Góngora? Is *Blood Wedding* a drama or a tragedy? These questions are addressed to the moderator, who expresses his intention of looking at reference works and consulting with others. When the group rejects his intention, he has to give his information and his opinion.

Overall, however, the process takes the monopoly of knowledge away from the coordinator and motivates people to use the resources and materials available to them in their own environments. Most have an encyclopedia at home and family members who will help them find answers. Adults spend little time in class, but there are plenty of educational situations in their everyday lives. The main goal is to learn, both in and out of the classroom. Following the path of dialogue, the group learns something about literature, but mostly how to learn.

The literary circle is made up of learning subjects rather than teaching objects: no absolute truths replace their own interpretations. Every explanation has the same formal value, although its influence depends on the information, reasoning, and reflection that it contributes. The debate does not force a dogmatic agreement with "the correct interpretation" or "the real truth." On the contrary, sharing different interpretations generates collective creations with human and literary meanings.

It is hard to reach this exercise of dialogical rationality and maintain it once achieved. The group is open to any type of visitor. It allows aspiring writers, who do not consider themselves members of the "gang" but select authors, to sit in on the readings and discussions. Rather than contributing dialogically to the group, they try to instrumentalize it, as if it were just another step towards their goal. Though they begin by speaking about the reading topic for the day, they take every opportunity to point out that they are writers, to read their poems, and sometimes even to sell their self-published works.

Gabriel, a teacher from a nearby adult education class, insistently proposed that they read his book; that way, they would have the opportunity to invite the writer (that is, himself) to be present at the discussion. The group's response was to invite him to come and read and discuss all of the books agreed upon. Gabriel declined, but then spent years criticizing La Verneda–Sant Martí's egalitarian and democratic project.

Early on in the literary group's existence, popular dynamics were confused with populism, dialogic rationality with instrumentalization of votes. Feeling that the people's voices had been silenced for too long, one educator from the center wanted to give all sorts of opportunities to those who, like himself, returned to study as adults. He founded a journal to publish texts written by participants. At first, very few people submitted items, but soon so many did that there was no way to deal with them all.

The selection process became an area of conflict. Deciding "democratically" by voting was even more problematic. Some people were upset with those who did not vote for their contributions. Others voted on a "you scratch my back, I'll scratch yours" basis. Some people took every opportunity to read their pieces aloud, forcing the rest to listen. At a party, someone actually stopped the music and jumped in front of the microphone to read some poems. The same thing happened at a conference and during conversations. This dynamic made people deaf to the other voices. From then on, the debates were oriented to overcome populism as much as to fight elitism.

Goyo believes that everyone can create texts without having to search for notoriety. A letter to a child or a friend can be of better narrative quality than a prize-winning book. It makes no sense to focus all energies on writing just to earn public recognition. The space created by commenting on and enjoying books could thus become a mere competition to establish which people are simply readers and which are also writers. There would even be the risk of reaching the populist criterion of applauding all poems equally, regardless of whether they are enjoyed or not.

The idea of giving literary value to daily experience has begun to be generalized. Reducing art to its commercialization, people fail to take into account the cultural richness generated outside of its confines. There are many incredible creations that will never be officially considered literature but that, nevertheless, significantly improve human communication.

DIALOGIC LANGUAGE

Seven people got together with Goyo to read and discuss texts. They were all participating in either literacy classes or new readers' classes. In spite of the enormous motivation and culture they had all shown in personal conversations, they had problems getting into higher academic level classes that would enable them to graduate. Their oral knowledge was far superior to the knowledge they could demonstrate in writing in the classroom.

Over the course of twenty years, more than three hundred people have participated in these gatherings. Twenty to thirty people meet once a week and can attend for as long as they wish. Most progress from a stage at which they read no books at all to a stage at which they devour works by Proust, Baudelaire, or Cortázar. The secret of this transformation is found within the people themselves. Their great abilities were given little social value until they came to the center, as they expressed themselves in different ways from those desired by academic authorities.

Calling the group a *tertulia literaria,* a literary circle, gives substantial weight to a recently invented activity. Participants did not know what a *tertulia* was at first, but soon received abundant information about it, especially from family members with more academic training. They found out that *tertulias* were intellectual conversations, generally held in cafés.

Goyo was afraid that this academic meaning might provoke undesired effects. He felt the language used might be counterproductive, forcing people into a strange territory. He proposed to base communication solely on dialogic language directed towards reaching an agreement among all participants.

Goyo did not suggest this in order to give classic content to the activity, nor did he hide his intentions behind the suggestion. The problem escaped him. The language pressured the group with intentions that, in the end, were condensed into two words: literary circle (*tertulia literaria*).

The group members decided to speak openly about the connotations of the concept: conversing and reading "high quality" literature. Most people wished to discuss the best works, but only as long as they were to their own individual taste. García Lorca was the key author in removing the distance between wishes and tastes. Reading his work turned difficulties into possibilities. Antonio, a Gypsy who made poetry with his guitar, gave light and sound to the sessions.

Lorca is considered by academics to be the best Spanish poet and playwright, the best writer after Cervantes. His books are "classics," and yet they are enjoyed more by people considered to be "illiterate" than by those with college degrees. Ordinary people's everyday lives and popular knowledge are more open to Lorca's images than are the lives and knowledge of scholars.

The first book the group members read by Lorca was *Gypsy Ballads.* The group became incredibly involved in the reading, reciting, and singing of the poems. From the moment she joined, Lola told many stories about the writer and other people from their hometown. The group members enjoyed the poetry rather than examining it scientifically. They followed the orientation of the poet, who considered himself unable to explain the meaning behind *Romance sonámbulo* [Somnambulist Ballad] because human beings, "through poetry, quickly approach the line where philosophers and mathematicians turn their backs in silence."

CONSENT AND DISSENT

People who visit the group learn and teach a lot; for example, one German educator who arrived while Nietzsche was being discussed made important contributions to the debate. However, some people get stuck behind the cultural communication walls; the sessions in which *Don Quixote* was debated provide one representative example.

Two college literature students came to a session, and one of them soon interrupted the conversation in order to explain the importance of Cervantes' work. Rather than talking it over, the student conveyed her university knowledge to people she regarded as having insufficient schooling. After speaking for several minutes, she began to explain that *Don Quixote* was a knight-errantry novel because Don Quixote only had books belonging to this genre. Suddenly, a chorus of voices rang out in disagreement; in chapter 6 of the first volume, the lady of the house, the niece, the priest, and the barber, rifling through Don Quixote's books to locate and burn any knight-errantry novels, find titles of all sorts.

In fact, all of chapter 6 is dedicated to a commentary on Don Quixote's books. Why did this student so resolutely affirm that Don Quixote possessed only knight-errantry novels? On the one hand, as a college student, she had heard and read a lot about the book, but perhaps she had never actually opened it herself. Then again, maybe she felt privileged in the group setting, surrounded by people with far less schooling than herself.

Her actions erected a cultural communication barrier: she replaced open dialogue with a "consensus" imposed from her higher status. But the group figured out how to demolish that barrier with its dissent, which was based on better reasoning. Faced with chapter 6, the two students opened themselves up to the group's contributions and abandoned their unconscious attempt to replace reasoning with academic authority.

Dialogic action needs consensus as well as dissent. All related theories and experiments emphasize the need for true consensus. But many also insist on the importance of dissent, including Paulo Freire, the followers of the tradition of cultural associations, and the members of the experimental La Barraca Theater Group.

Agreement is, of course, of the utmost importance in setting up guidelines that allow the group to exist in totally equal and libertarian conditions. But disagreement is also necessary. The existing norms are the result of insufficiently egalitarian agreements: these must be dissented from in order to reach others, the fruit of a better consensus. This was reached, for instance, when the participants rebelled against one of the habitual criteria: people with higher academic levels of training teach literature to the rest. But their disagreement is accompanied by reasoning, including the reading of chapter 6 of *Don Quixote*, which stimulates new and more equal agreements. There is another fundamental reason for dissent. We do not need to agree on everything, just on what we need to get by and to learn together. Other things can, and sometimes should, be seen in different ways.

The group enthusiastically debates the role of dialogic action in aesthetics, ethics, and knowledge. In aesthetics, the members agree to disagree because nobody has better or worse reasoning than anybody else: different strokes for different folks. It makes no difference whether or not people agree about literary preferences; conversing about different readings of texts, however, is positive, as individuals reveal where they agree or differ and include other people's considerations in their own reflections.

In considering ethics and knowledge, on the other hand, people tend to look for consensus through reasoning. With regard to García Lorca's assassination by Francoists or the influence of contemporary events in plays like *Blood Wedding* or *The House of Bernarda Alba*, information or reasons can be given that prove the truth of some interpretations and disprove others. In spite of what some had argued, for example, it was eventually agreed that the poet Luis Rosales tried, though unsuccessfully, to help Lorca. Lola contributed much to the defense of Rosales' good intentions, although Rosales perhaps made a mistake in bringing Lorca to a Falangist family. People agreed that there were connections between *The House of Bernarda Alba* and the real events in the house of Frasquita Alba, Lorca's neighbor, even though the real Alba had sons as well as daughters, unlike the character in the play. It was decided that a literary creation can recreate reality in order to penetrate more deeply into reality's most human dimension.

Consensus in ethical matters is also sought through reasoning. Lorca's possible homosexuality or his alleged falling in love with Dalí provoked many discussions. Maribel—who was born and lived in Fuente Vaqueros—claimed that it was part of a defamation plot from the right. Others thought they had enough information to maintain that it was true. In spite of these discrepancies, they reached an agreement on the ethical criterion: everyone has sexual freedom and can maintain relationships with whomever they wish, as long as the relationships are freely chosen by the parties involved.

INSTRUMENTAL AND DIALOGICAL LEARNING

Well-known authors consider instrumental and communicative learning to be in opposition to each other. At La Verneda–Sant Martí, however, dialogic learning includes any instrumental learning chosen by the participants. For example, some people want to stop being excluded from their family's erudite conversations; therefore, they want to learn a lot about the writers, their lives, influences, and historical contexts. These topics are regarded in the group as suggestions for dialogue.

In fact, the group's instrumental learning is developed more fully in this activity than in formally oriented courses with instrumental aims. The members learn more about literature in the group than their family members learn in school or college classes. The point is to respect and encourage all dimensions of learning, overcoming its two colonizations: technocratic, which eliminates communicative aspects; and populist, which omits instrumental aspects.

In a new readers' class, one teacher with technocratic aspirations insisted that they should "not waste time on banter and get down to the issues"; she thought that dialogic learning obstructed instrumental learning. She attributed the length of time José took to learn his multiplication tables to cognitive deficits which made him unable to do mathematics.

In their first conversation, José told Goyo that he was a traveling salesman. Many Gypsy salesmen are very good at mental calculations involving coins. José's cultural intelligence went unnoticed by the teacher because she did not want to "waste time" talking. Such technocratic colonization, aside from wasting time, created José's block when facing instrumental learning and led to his evaluation as cognitively deficient.

Some time earlier, Goyo had given classes at a place where the teaching staff, erroneously, used to call their method "dialogic education." When he arrived, one class had been dealing with the topic of unemployment for five straight weeks. He asked if the group had learned enough to be able to avoid being unemployed. They answered that his question implied a traditional perspective: giving students the technical knowledge needed to adapt to contemporary society, instead of transforming it.

Goyo was sure that such a teaching–learning perspective was very different from that proposed by Freire. The staff imposed the dialogue topics. Being civil servants, they decided that it was in the participants' interest to study unemployment; the students, on the other hand, living either in or in fear of unemployment, wanted to learn things that would help them get work or improve their job stability. They hoped to gain employment if they received instrumental training and a corresponding certificate. But that aspiration was looked down upon as "traditional" by staff members who, in order to acquire their own stable positions, had gone through higher instrumental training and received the necessary accreditation. Because they looked down on what participants felt and needed, the staff team at that center ended up denying, rather than practicing, dialogic learning.

Dialogic learning in the group promotes instrumental learning. Issues, feelings, opinions, and personal histories are all put forth and dealt with. People share this communication and learn a lot about literature, history, and art. But, fundamentally, they develop abilities like learning to learn and characteristics like self-confidence.

This process helps overcome all sorts of antidialogical barriers. Social barriers are surmounted, since neither teachers nor institutions are looking for power. Cultural barriers are overcome, because everyone is seen as creating meaning and participants' interpretations are valued by people with high academic qualifications. Personal walls are torn down because participants feel encouraged and gain strength from their own histories.

EMANCIPATORY LEARNING

Group action has a doubly emancipatory perspective: first, people are freed from the elite's oppressive monopoly of valuable words, and second, they open spaces in which to realize their emancipation. Often, emancipatory education was looked upon as part of a political struggle against the structures of the capitalist system. For example, using literature as a tool raised people's consciousness in strikes and demonstrations.

The literary circle's position is more global. Most people want to contribute to political transformation but, more important, they all want to improve their daily lives and relationships. Rather than using readings just to encourage movements for the distribution of material resources, the people want to defend and foster their own ways of living literature.

Lola gained a lot of self-confidence. She had always rejected educational authorities. First, she felt distanced from the academic way of thinking. Second, she had never accepted being separated from the classics or confined within the limits of what commercial systems consider mass culture.

Maybe having known García Lorca gave her subjective experience that reinforced her cultural communication. She began questioning the official interpretation of the poet and ended up mistrusting all of the dominant judgments. But for many years the expression of her opinions and passions had been almost totally repressed. In a cultural world colonized by power and commercial systems, even her peers underestimated her.

At the group sessions, Lola met people who valued her opinions and opened the door between everyday knowledge and select knowledge. She rejected the social prejudices that were based on that division. As Giroux proposes, she acted as a border crosser by refusing to be on one side of the barrier or the other. She joined a popular collective that also had a certain academic status: it belonged to an educational institution, there was a professor, and the members discussed the classics.

Lola felt important in the group. Her self-confidence was then transferred to other aspects of her social life. She became more independent from her husband and started going out with her daughter and then with friends of her own. Some years later she started to lose her sight. At that time she had already read many books and continued to participate actively in the group, though without reading the new books chosen. She overcame physiological limitations that would otherwise preclude learning for adults with low levels of schooling.

Lola tackled the problem, opening up new, alternative paths in adulthood and avoiding the pessimism of the lack of time or the feeling that "it's too late." She needed to learn and feel culturally sure of herself, and she did. The official story, written by people with years and years of schooling, excludes the contributions of people like those who have attended the literary circle. As long as we barricade our minds within the narrow confines of the academic world, we lose the multiplicity of interesting cultures created by people like Lola.

3

Chelo

Subject of Her Own Transformation

TRISTANA

Chelo was the prototypical "señora": a good wife and mother. In the late 1970s, she felt that the changing relations between men and women were destructive to traditional satisfaction. Often, "old-fashioned wives" seemed much happier than their daughters, who were involved in much more complex professional and personal lives.

Discussing *Tristana* started intense debates. The main character, who gives her name to the title, is a young woman in the custody of Don Lope, a friend of her dead parents. The group generally agreed that he used his image as protector in order to exploit the girl's innocence. They harshly criticized the sexist oppression that turned the hopeful girl into a tortured woman.

Most people sided with Tristana. They felt that Don Lope was a typical nineteenth-century Hispanic male and maintained that, deep down, every man harbors these attitudes, even if the current environment does not allow them to be manifested in the same way. Tristana was an example of a woman oppressed by sexism to the point of losing her personal identity. Some participants identified with the woman because they themselves were struggling at home with the powerful legacy of this type of thinking.

Chelo questioned this view, maintaining that "Tristana must see something in Don Lope or she wouldn't stay with him." She loves him in her own way; everyone has her or his own way of loving. She said that the relationships described in Pérez Galdós's novel were disliked by young people, but wondered: "Are the relationships they have today always better?"

The novel was made into a film. Before seeing it, the group was very much in favor of authors who challenged conservative figures in their works, such as Picasso's *Guernica*, Lorca's *Gypsy Ballads*, or Buñuel's *Un perro andaluz* [An Andalusian Dog]. But the group members had also developed critical abilities and did not always agree. They were unanimous, though, in feeling that Buñuel's film version of *Tristana* takes Don Lope's sexism to the extreme, making him an even more odious character than he is in the novel.

The works of the artists mentioned above formed the aesthetic and ethical values of intellectual critics during the last years of Francoism. During that period, Goyo went to a film forum on *Tristana*. The few people who attended saw Buñuel's films as an artistic criticism of the traditional bourgeoisie, the enemy of freedom. The fall of the dictatorship was seen as a new social context in which Tristanas would have opportunities to free themselves from Don Lopes. The film forums tended to conclude that women had to be made aware of the mistake they had made in accepting the roles given to them by conservative powers.

After ten years of democracy, Chelo was still one of those "mistaken" women who was totally unwilling to let other women change her views through a critical examination of books or movies. In addition, she disliked Buñuel's reading of the novel. In her opinion, the images, expressions, and tone of the film failed to show the love the two main characters felt for each other. She said that the view of traditional relationships portrayed made it difficult for young people to understand their elders.

Goyo's mind traveled through time and space during these sessions. Chelo's words made him compare the group's debate to the film forums. Passion was the most important difference. The group had read the book before seeing the movie; this is less often the case with intellectuals or students. The group members made their comments with emotion, based on experiences from their own lives. The ideas that sprang from their lips are never heard in the usual discussions of films and novels.

"LIBERATED WOMEN" AS CORRECT SUBJECTS

Chelo had one teacher who felt it was her duty to transmit her feminist consciousness to other women. Laia shared her liberating views with a group of women who were mostly "housewives." She considered them to be exploited by their husbands, their children, and patriarchal society in general, their exploitation including the language they used to define themselves.

These women worked all day at home and, in addition, sometimes cleaned other people's houses, in very insecure working conditions. Their husbands and children had circles outside of home, but they as wives were excluded from the social spaces outside the family. In some cases, they were also victims of physical abuse.

The affection between Laia and Chelo was as intense as their differences. Chelo also saw many problems in the lives of women who considered themselves "liberated." She felt that those young women had as much to learn as she herself did. Instead of imitating her teacher's model, she wanted to forge her own way. She said that real feminism had to be built up with contributions from all women.

Laia was born in Argentina; her family was exiled there after the Spanish Civil War. She returned to Barcelona in the mid-1960s, when she was twelve years old. She was familiar with the more important international liberation movements: movements for sexual freedom and solidarity with Vietnam, struggles against dictatorship, student rebellions, and feminist collectives.

Democracy's limitations disillusioned many activists. Solidarity with weaker groups was considered an unreal utopia, while priorities were oriented towards the acquisition of money and power. This was the end of the 1970s and coincided with a crisis in perspectives on liberation in Europe.

Some people gave up on their dreams and began to defend situations and aims they had previously attacked. Leaders of student revolts became corporative teachers. Laia became disillusioned with people who betrayed their egalitarian principles: they opposed the oppressors until they *became* the oppressors. She decided that students and intellectuals were of no use, and she joined poor neighborhood associations, becoming involved with adult education.

She still had the same principles as before, but now she was committed to those sectors of society that most needed egalitarian social transformation. The working classes and the unemployed were still suffering cultural inequalities, while student leaders were now doing just what they had been criticizing before. While many women were exploited in their own homes and the homes of others, professional progressives had them working in

undignified conditions, excluding them from the equal rights the progressives claimed to be defending.

Almost all women seemed to Laia to be Tristanas, and she wanted to help
them escape from their Don Lopes. Galdós's novel and Buñuel's film were
two important resources in the struggle, even if the women had trouble
understanding her message. The solidarity she felt made her refuse to use
her university education for her own individual benefit; she wanted to help
all women who lacked the means to discover first their oppression and then
the possibility of finding a better life.

"HOUSEWIVES" AS MISGUIDED OBJECTS

Laia's main objective was for the participants to be made aware of their
situation and of the possibility of transforming it. Her perspective was in
opposition to that of the dogmatic, inflexible movements that used the collective as an instrument of change with the promise of bettering the conditions of all oppressed people. As a radical feminist, she knew that these
totalizing proposals did nothing to rid women of inequality. She criticized
any indoctrination, whether it came from the left or the right.

She wanted the women to make decisions freely about their own lives.
She was convinced that by opening themselves up to new experiences with
more egalitarian relationships at home, they could improve their lives. She
felt she had the consciousness they lacked in their classes and saw it as her
responsibility to help them attain it.

Her viewpoint was situated within traditional modernity and based on
the subject–object dualism: herself as a transforming subject and Chelo as
an object to be transformed. The teacher–subject believed she possessed
the knowledge that the students–objects lacked, and she tried to convey it
to them in the classroom. Political parties saw themselves as bearers of the
truth with regards to the interests of the collectives–objects they claimed to
represent; if the objects did not agree, it was due to false consciousness.
Humans considered themselves to be the transforming subject of nature-
object and had an adequate model of progress with which to make the
transformation, even when this seriously threatened ecological balance.

Using books and films like *Tristana*, traditional modernist teachers explained the "correct" interpretation to their students. Progressive versions
denounced the chauvinism that locked many women inside masculine pris-

ons. Conservative versions focused on issues like the loss of family values, which led to the sexual abuse of the daughter of friends. Both, conservative and progressive, assumed the same responsibility: to teach the values and knowledge required to correctly understand the novel.

Laia wanted women to become protagonists of their own lives. But, used to being objects, they first had to become subjects by regaining their autonomy as human beings. She felt that this consciousness raising could facilitate the reflection needed in order to construct interpretations of novels like *Tristana*.

The idea of converting people–objects into subjects presupposed an important liberational perspective in the 1970s and an era of oppression in the 1990s. Why was Laia an autonomous subject and Chelo an object? Why did the teacher feel more feminist than the women who worked in the home? Later reflections and events proved that they were different rather than better or worse. The irony was in Laia's effort with Chelo: she tried to guide Chelo into self-guidance. New realities and social theories radically criticized the stances of traditional modernity.

DISSOLVING SUBJECTS

A key moment in Laia's descent from the position of "correct subject" came during a party at the center. She frequently identified with the daughters of participants in her classes, using them as examples of women with better and freer lives than their mothers. She was convinced they represented the liberation that all women would demand in the future. When she spoke to Chelo and her friend Luisa, their disagreements were as deep as the sincerity of their smiles, expressions of the affection they felt for people so different from themselves.

That night, Luisa was very worried about her daughter. There was a boy who was taking advantage of the daughter. She suffered because of it, but always gave in to him. He followed the "love 'em and leave 'em" school of thought, laughing about his conquests when he spoke with his buddies. The daughter's old boyfriend was still in love with her and his behavior represented all the egalitarian values the teacher defended and asked her students to demand from men. Luisa, however, was desperate: when the phone rang, her daughter only reacted if it was Don Juan on the line.

That was the straw that broke the camel's back. The conversation stirred

up some of Laia's already heated opinions even more. Laia had joined feminist movements that were full of values like equality, women's solidarity,
and antisexist sexuality. Year after year, her feminist companions abandoned those values and decided to do whatever they felt like. Some of
Laia's friends ended up treating good people just as badly as they accused
men of treating women. Others chose relationships with chauvinist men,
without realizing that they were being used as sex objects while the men
cheated on their wives, who were locked up at home.

In the end, Laia understood that she could not be the subject of anyone
else's transformation. She suffered as much from sexism as the "housewives" did, and while it was one thing to fight against it, it was quite another
to claim it had already disappeared. As her favorite feminist author, Montserrat Roig, said: "When the demonstration is over, we hide our purple
clothes under the bed."

Reaching that awareness had led to different paths for different people.
For Laia and some of her friends it meant the beginning of new and equal
relationships with many diverse women. The traditional modernist idea of
subjects and objects of transformation, consciousness raisers and raisees,
disappeared. The subject–object division was replaced with intersubjectivity, with dialogue.

Other women took opposing routes. They felt that egalitarian principles
limited their free will to do what they wanted. For instance, when they
picked up men who had wives locked up at home, they claimed that any
call for solidarity with those wives was repressive moralizing. They reacted
by attempting to dissolve, or destroy, the solidarist principles as well as
those subjects who defended them, that is, egalitarian movements and collectives. Laia said that such women closed women's circle of inequality:
women returned to the position of objects, and what is more, they did so
knowingly. It was impossible for her to accept that her friends could
change their practices, values, and theoretical references so radically. It
pained her to see them move from demanding castration for rapists to following writers like Foucault, who defends the depenalization of rape.

During the transition from dictatorship to democracy, Laia participated
in movements in which several teachers' unions were born. A long time
later, one professor raped a sixteen-year-old girl on a trip. Another male
teacher was sleeping in the same tent with a female student. The women's
section of a teachers' union made a public statement against the attack.

The next day, a press release from the same union discredited the women's group.

Don Lopes, rapists, and stalkers are found in traditional households but also in schools, discos, and all realms of social life. Laia's old friends had been members of the union that defended the attacker and his accomplices. Years earlier, they would have been the first to organize a demonstration to clarify the facts of the case. Now, the defense of their fellow corporate workers prevailed.

Of the six teachers on the trip, only one lost his job, and even he was simply transferred to another school. He was not the rapist, but he was the only teacher on the trip who did not have tenure. While the egalitarian and solidarist principles of the women's group in the union led them to denounce the attack, the corporative defense demanded that those principles, as well as the people and movements that supported them, be fiercely attacked. Often, those who fire the most radical attacks turn out to be what Habermas calls "renegades," that is, people who defend certain values and then later betray them.

SAPPHO OF LESBOS: INTERSUBJECTIVE DIALOGUE

In contrast to the disputes over *Tristana*, there was agreement on Sappho's poems. People as different as Laia and Chelo felt the same enthusiasm for the poetry of a woman who wrote about love and passion at a time when men wrote epics about heroes and wars.

There were more women than men in adult basic education classes. Administrators and intellectuals tended to attribute this to women's educational inadequacies. Throughout this insensitive, cultured society, scornful voices intoned with maddening insistence: "This is for bored housewives."

The angry response to this ignorant elitism sometimes fell into the trap of maintaining that other people went to the classes as well. This was close to stating that housewives have no right to education. Rather than criticizing the ignorant elitist statement on the grounds that other groups attend as well, we must reject its sexism. Many women work in their own homes as well as in other people's homes, including those of the insensitive know-it-alls who look down on them. These women are among the sectors of society that are doing the most to transform their lives; those sectors going through a process of change have always participated in adult education.

The people who make sexist declarations cannot see that they have much to learn from the social and educational dynamism of these women.

Laia and Chelo disagreed on many points, but they were spontaneously united in the feminist struggle for equal educational rights. They had read and talked about the fact that the first women's classes were founded by the Institución Libre de Enseñanza (Free Institution of Education), in the mid-1800s. Although they were held in a church, after mass, some newspapers fought the activities claiming that "they opened the doors of seduction." Only men could go out and study.

The group thought that the creation of a school twenty-six centuries ago was the true planting of a seed of utopia. Sappho was more progressive than many members of the artistic elite today. Since so little is known about her, the group feels free to imagine possible stories, which invariably link up with their own personal paths.

All of the women have their own epic: the achievement of their right to education. Though they might be considered misguided objects, together they develop a feminist liberation deeper than that of the subjects who try to raise their awareness. They have overcome great difficulties in order to study and are changing their own lives as well as the lives of their families, friends, and companions. They do it together because they are all subjects of their own existence, thanks to their relationships and dialogues with others. This intersubjectivity is the basis for their transformations.

Some texts say that Sappho was a lesbian and that the term comes from Lesbos, the city where she was born. This set off an argument whose conclusion was similar to that of the debate over Lorca's homosexuality, even though the group's membership had greatly changed between the first discussion and this one. It was impossible to reach agreement, but it was not necessary to do so.

What was agreed upon was the respect for diverse options, provided that all those involved had made their choices freely, that is, that their choices were the result of intersubjective agreement. To be a faithful "wife" like Chelo was different, not better or worse, than to be a liberated woman like Laia. The subject–object distinction of traditional modernism made no sense; no one had the right to consider herself the subject who should impose her will on the other, reducing her to a simple object. An even worse choice was to dissolve the subject, proposing that each individual should do whatever she could or whatever she wanted, thereby converting the egalitarian principles into false arguments to be destroyed or claiming that nothing is blameworthy, not even rape or abuse at home or on the street. Intersubjectivity, on the other hand, respects the options resulting from dialogue and rejects those imposed through violence.

Chelo and Laia have become transformers; they both subscribe to a liberation perspective, though in very different ways. Their mutual understanding and reciprocal respect have grown simultaneously. None of them tries to be like the other or to change the other. Each one wants to be her own island but part of the same archipelago.

SENSITIVE LITERATURE

As soon as I see you, I lose my voice, my tongue is tied, a subtle fire runs under my skin, I see nothing with my eyes, my ears buzz, sweat runs over me, I tremble beyond control; I am paler than wheat and appear almost dead.

—Sappho

The group members love this literature; it revives their most cherished memories. Thousands of years before they were born, Sappho was already expressing their feelings. The first writings on Western intimacy were written by a woman. Is the same true in other cultures? Chelo is quite certain that this is no coincidence. "Women are different; we feel love in a different way." The epics that men wrote at the time were about power; they spoke of violence, conquest, and achievement. In the midst of this bellicose landscape, a woman made her way with stories of love and emotion. Her characters are not ferocious assassins but sensitive humans.

The group prefers lyric to epic poetry, shared human sentiment to conquests of power. The women in the group have very different histories from those of men. They spend much of their time taking care of their families and are generally less competitive at work and in the struggle for representation, and even in games and sports. Their sentiments motivate them to read, think, and communicate. Violent books that are at the same time critical of brutality stimulate some of them, but they all reject narratives that dignify cruelty.

Sappho founded a women's school and, at the same time, created a body of work that was enormously different from the dominant literature of her time. From the moment they read her poems, the women in the group made her into the symbol of a deep aspiration: equality of differences. On the one hand, they are searching for equal educational rights so as to avoid their traditional exclusion from certain positions and groups; on the other, they want to be themselves and enjoy many traditionally feminine activities and attitudes. Their aim of being equally different is represented by Sappho's double action: founding a school was a pioneering move toward equality in educational rights; creating intimate literature marked the earliest known example of the struggle for women's right to be different.

Chelo had always disagreed with Laia over the feminism of equality that Laia had set forth in her consciousness-raising days. Chelo felt it was a form of pressure on women to try to be like men. The first time she heard people talk about a feminism of difference, she thought this would defend her ideas, her way of being, and her feminine activities. But she changed her mind when she found that some writers supporting this trend were in favor of prostitution. She read an article in an important newspaper arguing that being paid for sexual work was the same as being paid for administrative work.

She thought that Sappho would never have upheld such a position. The journalist spoke of disciplinary power, while Sappho wrote about feelings At a conference, some feminists of difference invited a prostitute to come and defend her position. Another feminist resolutely criticized this invitation: "There were slaves who opposed the end of slavery; some poor people sell their bodies for pharmaceutical experiments. Does that mean that we should consider being a slave or guinea-pig as fulfilling occupations as well?"

The women at the La Verneda center reject the idea of trying to become like men, which some feminists of equality seem to propose; but neither are they prepared to keep accepting—much less defending—sexist exploitation by men, as some feminists of difference do. They want to combine equality and difference, to have equal opportunities, but to use them in their own ways instead of in masculine ways. Some of the women call this perspective the feminism of equality of differences. In their opinion, Sappho took the same position many centuries earlier; her writings expressed her own free and equal spirit.

PENELOPE

Sappho awakened the group's interest in the presence of women in literature. One consequence of this at the center was the creation of another literary circle for works written by women. Chelo's group sought out female characters and came up with Penelope, Antigone, and the Trojan women. The proposed discussion of *The Odyssey* caused great debate. Its reputation as an important and difficult work generated conflicting opinions on whether to read it. After deciding to try, the group's interest grew with each turning page.

Penelope generated more interest than her husband. Ulysses is the kind of hero praised in men's literature. The group appreciated his human dimensions. They liked his rebellion against the attacks and injustices perpetrated by the gods. But he is cruel at times, as seen in the deaths of Penelope's suitors. One participant said that although such events are perhaps inevitable at certain times, it is not necessary to exalt them in art.

The group members are attracted by Ulysses' obsession with getting back to Ithaca, to his wife and son. At least that desire establishes a certain correspondence with his wife's faithfulness. To wait or not to wait is the central question, which the group had already seen in *The House of Bernarda Alba*, in relation to the mourning period. On that occasion it was easy to reach an agreement: they felt it was positive to move beyond a sense of obligation that was based more on what the neighbors might think than on love for a dead family member.

The debate over Penelope led to both agreements and disagreements. Everyone was against traditional waiting periods; many women had waited for years for their husbands to return, knowing nothing about their husbands' new relationships abroad, not even receiving a letter. They unanimously rejected this unilateral type of relationship. When a relationship was reciprocal, however, and when communication existed, they valued it.

The disagreements arose when they started to discuss Penelope's actions, which reminded them of what had happened frequently after the Spanish Civil War. Two sides emerged: reject social pressure when you do not know if the man will return or even if he is alive; have faith unless you have evidence to the contrary. "In the history of wars and emigration, there have been many deceived Penelopes," most said. "But there have also been many happy reunions," said Chelo.

Some women strongly defended the first stance: ten years with no news is too long. Ulysses is always looking out for himself, while his wife weaves all day and secretly unweaves at night; finishing the veil would mean accepting a suitor. Chelo would do the same. In her opinion, Penelope acts that way because she is really in love and her husband is the man of her dreams.

Going with another man would be the sacrifice. Ulysses is seen to be faithful to his wife because he fights in order to return to her. Chelo is sure that her husband would have done the same.

Lola states that, luckily, young people now reject the role of Penelope. Chelo replies by telling the recent story of Cecilia Orlandi, a sixteen-year-old girl who lost hope when her sweetheart went into an apparently irreversible coma. It was then discovered that Cecilia's love registered on the hospital monitors. Her boyfriend's heart beat faster whenever she spoke to him. Four years later he began showing signs of coming out of the coma and, finally, the doctor said he might recover. The boy's mother said that Cecilia had kissed her son so many times while he was in the coma that she couldn't count, but that she could see how, day by day, it had saved his life. Chelo concludes that love, true love, always has been and always will be stronger than distance or science.

DIALOGUE BETWEEN FRIENDS

Laia and her friends are idealists. Some of her friends have extramarital relationships but do not consider themselves unfaithful because their lifestyles are respectful of their spouses and their sexual freedom is mutually agreed upon. One of them criticized the traditional idea of faithfulness: the idea that it does not matter how much or how little you love your partner, as long as you do not love anyone else. Instead, she feels that faithfulness means loving, even giving your life for your partner, rather than rejecting the possibility of loving other people.

By reading Sappho and becoming friends with Laia, Chelo comes to understand these feelings, although she does not share them. She understands that they are based on love and fidelity. Laia has also been able to see that Chelo's ideas are based on warm feelings. The feminist realizes that the "conservative housewife" makes decisions that are at least as valid as her own for the emancipation of women.

The two came closer to agreement on *Trojan Women*. While their husbands were off in search of glory in battles, the Trojan women stayed home crying over the war. They were motivated by what Laia, before she met Chelo, would have called traditional values. Thanks to her friend, the teacher realized that love and fidelity were values for all times, to be included in any progressive perspective. Laia and Chelo share the same desires for liberation, each according to her own ideas and feelings.

During the Balkan war, Laia became a peace activist, joining groups supporting the international intervention that the Bosnians wanted. Her humanitarian commitment made her unable to remain passive during the genocide. The use of rape as a weapon intensified her feelings.

Every day, Chelo became more and more affected by the destruction of families caused by the war. Certain words were sacred to her: home, husband, daughters. She rebelled against the shots that were fired, killing families. One day, the Miss Sarajevo candidates paraded wearing the slogan "Don't let them kill us." A year later, Imela Nogic, the winner, was killed by a sharpshooter. People from very diverse backgrounds, like Bono and Pavarotti, recorded a song that sadly referred to this death, saying she was just a child, a girl. Listening to Pavarotti, Chelo thought the girl could have been her daughter. Listening to Bono, Laia thought of one more victim of a cruel war. The two women were united in their feelings of powerlessness and indignation.

4

➤➤

Rocío

Overcoming Ageism

AGEISM

Between you and me, it might be true that a college education cannot compete with folklore, with popular knowledge. Ordinary people know more and, generally, better than we do.

—Antonio Machado

This statement revolutionized Rocío's educational picture of herself. Until then, she had always seen herself as the "cultural elite" sees her, as a person with significant educational deficits. Machado's mirror, on the other hand, reflects the image of a woman of the people, with much to teach intellectuals.

You can choose between many different images. Elitists, although they are less cultured than Machado, underrate people like Rocío. The mirrors that show the reflection of an uncultured woman belong to those who only pretend they are superior, not to truly cultured people.

Elitist mirrors excluded Rocío with their assumption that she was too old to study. She knew about ethnic and sexual discrimination, but not age discrimination; everyone spoke about racism and sexism, but ageism was new to her, although it was the primary reason for her exclusion.

In class there was a lot of discussion of an idea that used to be common before feminism questioned gender roles: girls should not play football and boys should not play with dolls. Men opposed ethnic or class-based discrimination, but still held on to their chauvinism. These sexist ideas set up an insurmountable barrier between men's and women's activities.

One teacher said that the same thing applied to ageism. Barriers were set up separating off all of the activities considered "appropriate to each age group." Basic education was just for children and teenagers. Progressives fought against racism, sexism, and classism, but accepted the ageism that denied learning opportunities and equal educational rights to people of different ages.

Rocío went to school until she was nine. When her family moved to Barcelona, her sister Charo continued going to school but Rocío was put in charge of the family chores, while her mother sewed for a local tailor. She held back her tears when she remembered what she was doing at the age of ten, instead of going to class. "Take the pot off the stove when it starts boiling." "Mom, what's boiling?" "Well, let me know when it starts making little bubbles."

If Rocío bought clothes, she always chose those that most resembled Charo's school uniform. That way she secretly felt that she was more closely linked to school, and she planned to save the clothes until she could go. She was very excited about getting a blue cardigan; now she had almost everything. On the day she turned fourteen she got out of bed overcome with hopelessness, sure that she was too old ever to go to school. That same day she lost her cardigan.

She began to work in a tailor's shop. Years later she decided to go to night classes put on by the Sección Femenina (Francoist Women's Section), but she soon gave up. Instead of learning, as they would at school, the women only chatted and played. Besides, Rocío had to wait on the street before the class, and she did not like that. Later, she tried out three different private institutes, but she found the atmosphere too much like elementary school and she felt them inappropriate for a person of her age.

When she was thirty-two, she heard someone talk about a new adult education center. In the shop where she worked, they often had the radio on. That day, on a local station, a group of participants from La Verneda–Sant Martí were explaining the educational activities of the center. Rocío thought she would never become an academic, but she did, at least, want to complete her basic schooling. Within a hierarchical conception of culture, based on levels, she felt that she would always be inferior to those who had studied when they were adolescents.

AGEIST EDUCATION

In the late 1970s there was a renaissance in adult education, but the 1980s saw the birth of attacks on popular adult education projects. New ageist barriers were being erected. Some teaching faculty members actually closed their doors to people over sixty-five. Others refused to allow people to continue if they had not reached a certain level within two years. The fundamental problem was prejudice against presumed learning limitations. Often people thought that all those in literacy education would be incapable of finishing their basic mandatory schooling, or that, if they finished, they would never get to college.

One of Rocío's classmates, Lucía, directly experienced the difference between a setting where people have confidence in everyone's cultural intelligence and one where many people are excluded due to prejudices like ageism. She signed up at La Verneda because it was close to her work, while her mother went to another center close to home.

Lucía wanted to begin the highest course of basic education, but she did not achieve a high enough score on the entrance exam. The first year, she passed the pre-basic level; the second year the basic level; the third year the university entry exam for over twenty-fives for the university. Five years later she got her degree.

Things did not go so well for her mother. After spending two years on the same course, she was ordered to leave the basic education course and sign up at a leisure workshop. The right to education was therefore withdrawn, shattering the dreams she had nurtured for so long. Often, while she cleaned the house, she imagined herself overcoming her exclusion from conversations, understanding her daughter's scholarly language, and making her own friends outside her home.

Ageism got in the way of her dreams and desires. Her mental blocks were interpreted as a result of "already being too old," "not having done it in time," and "diminished capacities." Scientific theories and emancipatory proposals maintained that adults had unexplored learning abilities. The ageist teaching staff, however, said those theories and proposals did not take day-to-day practice into account and that, in the long run, such utopian ideas would only lead to deeper frustrations when the harsh truth was uncovered.

Lucía's mother lost a golden opportunity to increase her self-esteem and to learn. Instead of being a liberating experience, the time spent at an educational center internalized and intensified her sense of exclusion. She was happy for her daughter's progress, but even that happiness reinforced her ageist conceptions: "It worked out for [my daughter] because she is only twenty-four." Lucía knew the error of that stance firsthand because in La Verneda other women the same age as her mother were making extraordinary advances in their education.

AGEIST CONCEPTIONS

Goyo wants to escape the ageism of his academic environment. His is the only career that means spending one's whole life in the same setting. Doctors, journalists, and waiters all go to school first and then on to hospitals, newspapers, and restaurants. Teaching faculty spend their first years in school and then . . . stay in school until they retire. There are also large numbers of "pedagogical" marriages and friendships within the profession.

When you are teaching, you forget that you know little about your specialization and almost nothing about anything else, but you do think that the students lack basic knowledge. Goyo often does an experiment. He asks a team of teachers to write down what each of them feels should be the minimum requirements needed to obtain a school diploma in their own subjects, the bare minimum necessary in order to function adequately in society. Professors then realize that they do not know many of the answers. The social science teacher includes the names of the countries of the European Union on the list of requirements, and the literature teacher does not know them. The math teacher suggests a minimum requirement that the social science teacher cannot meet. Of course, each member of the teaching team has a university degree and a secure job in teaching.

With adults who had been excluded from education, though, people used Wechlser's ageist explanations or misapplied Piaget's theories to adulthood. From this perspective, the people in the literary circle were either girls who needed to develop cognitively (Rocío) or else deficient adults who had missed the boat (Lucia's mother).

The members of one sector of the teaching bureaucracy presented themselves as experts on everyday practice, scoffing at theory because "it is so far from reality." Without knowing it, they were basing their teaching on deficit theory. They thought that people who did not correspond to the model of Western, educated boys lacked ability and motivation to learn. They threw into that category not only adults attending basic education classes but also Mahgrebi and Gypsy children.

For the team at La Verneda–Sant Martí, the real problem is not the difference between theory and practice, but the difference between good and bad theory and good and bad practice. Theories and practices of poor quality reinforce educational exclusion. High-quality theories and practices move beyond that exclusion.

Professionals and participants in adult education challenge the theories that exclude a large part of humanity from their equal right to learning. The research that has moved beyond deficit theories has not been sufficient to remove the stigma that exclusionary theories have placed on Rocío. But the readings and literary discussions have managed to achieve what the scientific theories Goyo studied could not do on their own.

THE FREE INSTITUTION OF EDUCATION

Rocío loves Machado. Reading *Juan de Mairena* furthered her education. The author tells the pedagogical story of Abel Martín and his student, Juan de Mairena, recalling the atmosphere that he himself had encountered as a student at the *Free Institution of Education* (ILE). Rocío's experience at La Verneda–Sant Martí was different from her previous ideas about education. In this book she discovered how important thinkers had elaborated similar methods.

Abel Martín complains: "Every day literature is written more and spoken less, and the result is that every day it is written worse." In the group, Rocío found spoken literature. From that moment on, she stopped caring about whether or not the center's way of teaching was the same as in schools.

In the passage that Rocío remembers best, the author says that teachers should direct themselves towards the less-advantaged students and make it clear that they are speaking to them. In the pre-basic school level class, different people were mixed together. Some, like Rocío, came from the new readers' class. They tended to feel less prepared than the others. Rocío invented strategies to get people to notice her. She thought the most effective one was to open her eyes very wide, so that the teacher, while presenting an explanation, would see how attentive she was and look right at her. She said some days her facial muscles hurt when she got home, but it was worth it if it meant that the teacher did not pay attention solely to the same students all the time.

Machado was a high school teacher himself and the Free Institution of Education was generally involved in the extension and improvement of the school system. But far from restricting education to childhood, as if that were the only proper time for learning, he was committed to adult education. At that time, there was a scarcity of research into adulthood and adult education. But Machado always valued popular knowledge and the abilities of older people.

Rocío agreed with Machado about the importance of everyday knowledge, but she also wanted to gain academic knowledge. She left the Women's Section classes because they were useless in terms of gaining any knowledge she considered "cultivated." *Juan de Mairena* values popular culture but also "superior knowledge." To gain either one, direct and egalitarian dialogue between people from different spheres is necessary.

The discussion of Machado's book led the group to become interested in the Free Institution of Education. They discovered the poet's link to a generation of writers and artists who made Spain culturally far more important than the country's international economic and political importance might have suggested. Machado, Picasso, García Lorca, Buñuel, Dalí, and Blasco Ibáñez all belonged to this generation.

Long before, when Spain was of great military importance, another generation of internationally influential writers and artists arose. Cervantes, Velázquez, and Lope de Vega all lived in the days of the "empire where the sun never sets." The country that dominates the world is the one with the most influential intellectuals. Deficit theories are applied to the others, thereby declaring their cultures inferior.

Picasso, Buñuel, and Lorca used their works to break out of this exclusionary logic. One reason for this might be found in the Free Institution of Education, in terms of the caliber of its students, the activities developed in the "Residencia de Estudiantes," and the relationships formed there.

The artists and writers of the Free Institution, along with politicians, entrepreneurs, and others, constituted an elite. But they also kept in very close contact with popular culture and popular movements. They collaborated on excellent projects in poor areas, working-class neighborhoods, rural villages, and mining towns. Blasco Ibáñez founded the first popular university in Valencia; Machado worked on the Pedagogical Missions Foundation; García Lorca took cultural communication to different towns with his La Barraca theater group.

Unfortunately, in the first years of La Verneda's literary circle, the majority of intellectuals seem to have harbored quite different feelings. Popular knowledge was undervalued, even openly scorned. One intellectual who became quite popular during the year of Barcelona's Olympic Games even declared on television that he thought adult education was worthless because, since children were the future, everything should be invested in the school system. (However, he even "forgot" to ask that the public funds he was receiving should also be used for artistic training in children's schools.) Perhaps he felt that his works were culture, and adult education centers were just a waste of time.

La Verneda–Sant Martí's transformative perspective changed that situation. Among other things, for example, the center established "Seven to Eight." At seven minutes before eight o'clock, sessions were held in which a particular author's work was discussed. Sometimes up to five hundred people attended. Among those who generously gave of their time were José Luis Aranguren, Teresa Pàmies, and José María Valverde. They all agreed: the audience was unique in its enthusiasm and in its composition of people normally excluded from such gatherings.

TRANSFORMING EDUCATIONAL AGEISM

Participants were deeply disappointed by certain intellectuals' and politicians' statements attacking adult education. They could not understand how well-known authors were so ignorant on the subject and, in particular, how they dared to pontificate in the media about things they knew nothing about. It was so disturbing that participants ended up actually doubting their own opinions.

Especially in those moments of insecurity, the importance of readings and literary discussions can be seen. The ideas of people like Machado give the group authority over artists whose cultural status is superior to its own but inferior to that of the poet from Seville. Speaking about these matters enriches and reinforces people's convictions and their transformative will. The group tries to convert its popular knowledge into scientific theories and practical actions. Its members help adults regain the dignity so long denied them by educational and social theories.

One educational reform project based the treatment of adults on an age-ist concept. It said: "When general or basic education is not acquired by the appropriate age, action must be taken to compensate for this." The group decided to examine the two fundamental aspects of this idea: compensation and appropriate age.

The group's experiences were at odds with the idea of reducing basic education to compensation for what was not attained during childhood. Many people finished school as teenagers and yet still lacked what is considered basic schooling today. The explanation was so simple that the group members could not believe intellectuals and politicians could not see it.

The more advanced information society becomes, the greater the training required. Educational reforms raise the level of education required for a diploma. Adults who completed the requirements as teenagers therefore still have a lower level of education than people going to school now. In other words, the reforms produce an *unleveling effect* on adults.

So hard for the experts to see and so obvious to those who are suffering as a result of the situation. If only the experts had asked questions before writing their new books and laws! Those who finished their basic schooling before 1990 were going to find that the new law established higher educational requirements. Therefore, before 1990 they were up to the required standard and afterwards below the standard. That means that the information society's advances and school reform reclassify these people as educationally deficient. In order to reach the required educational level, they have to go back to school and get another diploma. Those in charge of the new reform thought that, little by little, the number of adults with no compulsory education diploma would decrease; they did not realize that in actual fact, the movement was in the opposite direction.

In addition, the "appropriate age" prejudice ignores the abilities of adults. The offer directed at adults, therefore, concentrates on their hypothetical deficiencies, leading to low learning expectations. Allowing that idea to be included in the framework of all educational reform legislation would have implied perpetuating an erroneous educational policy for many years.

The group often talks about all the things adults learn in their social circles, regardless of their years of schooling. The members also discuss the alarming inability of academic mentalities and institutions to perceive that learning. Many traveling saleswomen who get stuck when they do addition exercises in an academic setting actually multiply perfectly in the market. Waiters who cannot remember what year they were born easily remember the list of drinks customers order. People who do not know the year in which Spain began its transition to democracy are able to explain in great detail many events that occurred at the same time.

How could we convince society that all ages are appropriate for learning? How could we make them see the ageism and lack of scientific validity of their exclusionary ideas? Scientific status had to be given to popular knowledge. Sylvia Scribner's studies on practical intelligence and research on cultural intelligence developed by the team who would later form the Center for Social and Educational Research (CREA) helped to provide such scientific status. Thus, ideas from popular knowledge could be accepted as scientific theories rather than being rejected paternalistically as "simple, practical intuition of humble people."

La Verneda–Sant Martí adult education center was consulted by the promoters of the educational reform project mentioned above, and the center's position was accepted. The project's next document replaced ageist concepts with others open to adult learning. For example, the aforementioned paragraph was replaced with this: "An essential foundation is the general or basic education which, ever wider and more demanding, is required for adults to be able to function in our evolving society." The section of the final text of the law dedicated to adult education was based on these new concepts.

FUENTEOVEJUNA

Reading *Fuenteovejuna*, the group was moved by the town's solidarity with the lovers, Laurencia and Frondoso. They unite to face the king commander's power, when he wants to exercise his *droit de seigneur* with Laurencia. Popular passion overcomes the commander's contemptible oppression and is mixed with enthusiasm because the townspeople are rebelling against women's grueling exploitation.

Lope de Vega's work brings together very different people—those who are normally for such rebellions and those who are normally against them—united in their support of antiauthoritarian action They are all equally indignant over the king commander's aggression. Often in La Verneda–Sant Martí, people who vote for different political parties and think in different ways find themselves united, through dialogue, on aims they all consider to be just.

The center suffers from the same contradictions as society. Internal power relations create tension. One group of teachers who had defended popular movements when they were in insecure working situations later attacked them when they got tenure. Their old ideals (emancipatory perspectives and solidarity) were now restraining their new individual and corporate aspirations, especially if the old ideals affected these teachers' power over participants.

As part of their social activity, faculty members had struggled against the bureaucratic norms that created problems when it came to organizing themselves around adult needs. They made fundamental changes in schedules and curricula, facilitating class attendance and empowering adult learning. The population's needs and motivations were the main guide in the new educational organization.

At La Verneda, as in other places, employees work according to the participants' needs. From the start, there have been four class times: 9:30 to 11:30 A.M., 3:00 to 5:00 P.M., 5:30 to 7:30 P.M. and 7:45 to 9:45 P.M. The first class is convenient for people who work afternoon or night shifts, or for people who work from home. The last one is the only possibility for people who work in both the morning and the afternoon.

After some years, certain members of the faculty began to think more about their own interests than those of the neighborhood. Autonomy and organizational flexibility are two good examples. A conflict erupted when a section of the faculty changed the class schedules. In the new schedule, many of the 7:45 to 9:45 P.M. classes disappeared, which meant that almost everyone who worked mornings and afternoons could no longer attend. Classes were scheduled from 9:00 to 11:30 A.M., and from 11:30 to 1:00 P.M., making it almost impossible for anyone with school-aged children to attend.

The schedule was impossible for the participants but very convenient for the faculty members who made the decisions. If faculty members were dependent on a playschool for child care, they taught every day from 9:00 A.M. to 1:00 P.M. and one afternoon a week from 3:00 to 5:00. If they went to college in the mornings, they taught every day from 3:00 to 7:30 P.M. and just one evening from 7:45 to 9:45.

Instead of ensuring that the center and its staff were at the service of the participants, the members of this section of the faculty modified the organization so that it was at their own personal and corporative service. Flexibility and autonomy, the victories of the people, were aggressively overturned.

People opposed this exclusion. But it was not quite the same situation as in Lope de Vega's play. In *Fuenteovejuna*, the commander is a character who stands out because of his evil characteristics and has no influence over the audience; he is the "bad guy" in the movie. At La Verneda–Sant Martí, the oppression came from real people with links and influence. Besides, their opponents did not want to hurt the oppressors, they just did not want them to hurt the sixteen hundred participants.

The representative assembly decided to keep the scheduled times the same as in previous years, with the support of participating associations, neighborhood organizations, and the rest of the professionals. They asked the administration to get rid of the corporative sector of the faculty, given their negativity towards dialogue and the democratic process.

As in *Fuenteovejuna*, the rebellion at La Verneda had a happy ending. The administration removed the corporatist sector and the center enjoyed excellent participation, democratic proceedings, high educational quality in adult learning, and the defeat of ageism in the following years. Seeing the decrease in corporate interests and the increase in human ideas, people said: "Educational centers would be more attractive if they had fewer Sancho Panzas and more Don Quixotes."

The literary group went to see *Fuenteovejuna* performed by Antonio Gades's theater group. Rocío, who is Andalusian, was incredibly moved by the performance. Her admiration increased during the scene with the washerwomen: she said that the ballerinas were most expressive without words, just moving like white sheets. She did not feel like a passive object of the performance; she herself had recently taken part in a popular rebellion similar to the one staged in the theater. That night, when she went to bed, she felt very satisfied with the life she now led.

5

Juan

Decolonizing Everyday Life

THE REVOLUTION OF *METAMORPHOSIS*

After the group had read and sung poems, when suggestions were sought for a first novel to be read, Goyo included Kafka's *Metamorphosis* as one of the possibilities. People with high academic qualifications who had come to know the group were very surprised, as they considered it too difficult for beginners. But two things attracted group members from the start: the book was short and the print was big. Those who started to read it quickly felt an electrifying connection between Gregor Samsa's miscommunication with his family and the feelings they themselves had experienced since moving from rural villages to modern, literate cities.

The participants felt quite disturbed by the book. Every day, Gregor gets up to go to the office, but one morning he cannot get up, since he has turned into a large insect. His mother is horrified when she sees him. His father threatens him with a cane, ignoring the pleading he does not understand. His sister Grete accepts the change with resignation but, little by little, begins to see Gregor more as an insect and less as a brother. Eventually, she feels liberated when she finds him dead.

People who read the book are directly, intimately, in touch with the protagonist's feelings. They know that he is still the same human being, and now even more sensitive than before. But the rest of the characters, deprived of literary contact, are aware only of his animal exterior and not of his human interior.

The family members treat their son and brother more and more like an insect, while the readers' attitudes towards Gregor evolve in anxiety. Kafka brings out all the drama of everyday family life. The book casts doubt upon what we take for granted, what we avoid questioning: our daily lives.

In the rural areas the participants come from, meaning used to be externally affirmed. The traditional family filled the private space, and the Catholic Church created meaning in the public sphere. Everyone was a member of society and attended mass, the central activity in town, on Sundays. There were three defined authorities: the doctor, the teacher, and the priest. The doctor made decisions about the body, the teacher about the mind, and the priest about the soul. Their invisible powers were intimately tied in with their very visible personalities.

Gatherings on the street, in the afternoon, were open dialogues, with no guide or schedule; all you needed to participate was a chair. Weddings, funerals, stories, legends, games, jokes, and refrains were all viewed through these direct and face-to-face relationships, which were part of community life. Popular culture, ballads, natural home remedies, and a lot of other rich, collective knowledge was intimately linked up with these conversations. Adult education was born out of these dialogues.

The social landscape is very different in cities. Only a few people in the neighborhood go to church on Sundays. No one pressures those who do not go, because society does not consider religious practice an obligation. One of the things people gain with migration is freedom, in the sociological sense of a plurality of choices. One of the disadvantages is the loss of meaning, since rural religiosity is not replaced by any other response to spiritual concerns.

Power over bodies, minds, and souls went from visible people to anonymous systems. The doctor was replaced by the health system; the individual making the diagnosis was much more a doctor than a person. Patients saw him or her only in the health care center and not walking around the town with his or her family. The teacher was replaced by the educational system; the teacher was still an authority in the classroom, but no longer in the community, in which he or she did not live or else was just another anonymous neighbor. The priest was replaced by a television which, like God beforehand, could be found everywhere and was present as an image in the heart of every household.

Conversations on the street were also replaced. Sayings, jokes, and stories were replaced by the mass media. Open spaces disappeared. The whole neighborhood watched the same television channel, but each family watched within the four walls of its own home. Inside the houses, people sat together, but rather than sitting face-to-face, all faced the television.

The increasing rejection Gregor experienced from his family when he most needed them made participants reconsider key elements in their daily existence, things they had previously taken for granted. What would happen to their lives if they were suddenly paralyzed or caught a contagious disease? What if they became so old they could not take care of themselves anymore? How would people react? How would they themselves act if the same thing happened to a member of their family or a friend?

In general, they neither entirely condemned nor entirely condoned the behavior of Gregor's family. Instead, they understood both sides of the story. Rather than seeing good or evil in the characters, they saw a problem in the conditions of the characters' lives and their communication that was related to love and solidarity. *Metamorphosis* was an emotional milieu, a passionate mirror in which the literary circle participants discovered new ways to describe their own existences. Written words offered delicate reflections on their family ties. Uncertainties were mingled with the satisfaction of feeling respected and protected by their loved ones. All the members of the group became much more sensitive in their relationships.

Most professionals do not believe Goyo. They have trouble picturing *Metamorphosis* as one of the most thrilling choices for people with limited prior scholastic opportunities who are taking up reading and discussion. They underrate the collective and cannot see that when people read from their own perspectives, each page reveals profound dimensions of their beings. Whether or not they like the plot, the participants are hooked on the reading; they not only discover "great works of universal literature," they also uncover hidden aspects of their own lives.

Passionate is perhaps the best word to describe the debates, given that no one remains indifferent in the sessions. Passion for *Metamorphosis* leads to passion for literature. However, in the first group that read it, Goyo detected that one person was very uncomfortable. First this person stopped speaking, and then he stopped coming to the gatherings. The discussion of Kafka's book had made his awareness of his family problems even more acute. The coordinator saw this as the first of his own failures; in part because he was unaware of the problem before the debate began, and then because he had not planned for the possibility of anything of the sort happening.

SPACES FOR CONVERSATION

The group members' enthusiasm for *Metamorphosis* led to other Kafka works. For months, they considered the possibility of reading *The Trial.* In the end, because it was already so "famous," they decided to give it a try. A troubling lack of meaning began to crop up in discussions. At first people wanted to guess who was after Joseph K, what he was accused of, and how he would end up. Little by little they got to know a protagonist who was himself desperate because he could not find the answers to these same basic questions.

Joseph K was as lost in his life as the group was in the book: none of them knew what he was accused of or by whom. The reading made them feel close to the character, sharing their common desperation at being unable to make sense of events. As they progressed, they began to realize that even the end of the book would not answer their questions. The narration remained as unfinished as the trial it described.

To escape the feeling of absurdity that overcame them, the group members began to construct their own interpretations of the reading and of Joseph K's life. The discussions led them to draw a parallel between his defenselessness against unknown authorities who controlled him like a puppet on a string and the everyday defenselessness of people facing bureaucracy in modern urban societies.

In rural areas, authorities had eyes and faces. Decision makers were known to the people. In industrial cities, immigrant groups encountered an administration whose decisions were made by anonymous bodies following unexplained procedures. The aim seemed to be for no one to understand so that no one could complain. Everything was justified with the mysterious sentence, "Those are the rules."

Most of the group was born in small towns, collectives bound together by the relationships between their inhabitants. Now on the outskirts of urban areas, the group members feel that society is made up of impersonal structures. Based on those feelings, they can share Joseph K's feelings of impotence and disorientation, although they feel less isolated than he does.

On the one hand, bureaucrats' decisions make them lose their sense of community; the "come back tomorrow" they hear in various institutions is similar to the repeated postponement of the end of Joseph K's trial. On the other hand, they are rebuilding the meaning of their daily lives with new family, neighborhood, and commercial interactions.

The literary gathering is a part of that reconstruction. Some people find there the satisfaction they used to feel in the open air, casual conversations back in their home towns. Their motivation for participating is linked to the sound of words, of talking things over. Unfortunately, that desire remains unsatisfied in many classes, since traditional models of participation are closed to many voices and require people to be quiet. One humorist summed up what often occurs: "Quiet please, language class is about to start." The norms of the school system put up barriers to communication: chatting must stop when class begins.

That silence leads people to look for other places for conversation. Bars and markets are places for conversing, while in some classrooms you have to be quiet. People go to bars to eat or drink but also to chat; often, a drink is just an excuse to accompany conversation.

Families who migrated from the country to the city saw their public and private spaces inverted. From big, spacious houses in the country they moved to occupy one-bedroom apartments in buildings where three or four other families already lived. In those conditions, the goal was to get their own place, large or small, where married couples could have their own bedrooms.

The speculators who built the commuter suburbs "forgot" about public space. People who were used to intense community relationships were shut away in small apartments. Many men found new social worlds in factories and bars. Most women looked to markets and stores. Young people used schools and discos.

Places for conversation evolved with social transformations. In Barcelona, one of the unexpected consequences of the feminist struggle was the development of a popular women's movement in "granjas," which are a type of cafeteria where many women go for a while after dropping their children off at school. There they speak about clothes and their children's studies, food and hair salons, their relationships with their partners and equal rights, friendship and solidarity, work and fun, politics and culture. At the literary group meetings, people call these gatherings "the farm's revolution," which is a play on the Spanish title of Orwell's *Animal Farm* (as the word "granja" has two meanings: a farm and a cafeteria).

Until then, those women only went to cafés or bars with their husbands. If they wanted to speak among themselves, they did so only at the market or at the school gates. The intense interaction created at the "granjas" has transformed their interpretations, actions, and ideas. The changes include their massive educational participation. They want to learn and speak; that desire challenges the barriers to communication produced in classrooms that were spaces for being quiet.

Neighborhood movements also represented an important source of new places for conversing. They provided associations, cultural centers, parties, social services, and sports centers. At first men used to speak about football, women, and politics in bars. Then, men and women talked about social or educational topics in associations. Later, though, men and women all came to speak about everything, everywhere.

Participation fails when that dynamic is opposed, instead of roots being put down to empower it. The literary circle, as a space for conversing, takes on many of the communication aspects found in the "granjas"; but some women also take the literary and social issues discussed in the group to the cafeterias.

SPACES FOR SILENCE

The participatory dynamic explodes the conservative structures that define who has and who lacks knowledge. From their positions of power, the members of the elite deny common people the ability to create meaning. Elite members dislike the fact that a huge increase in participation means their own "ingenious" ideas are no longer revered. They continuously invent new reasons to silence popular creativity.

Goyo has always felt like just another member of the people. He does not consider his academic knowledge to be more creative or more valuable than the knowledge other people in his neighborhood have. While he was in college, he worked one summer in a grocery store with Nati, a girl his age who had left her studies years earlier to get a job. In order to get to Bilbao from La Arboleda every day, they had to go by funicular railway and by train. Of the books Nati read on the way to and from work, Goyo had only read plot summaries and studied the lives of the authors. She was the cultured one, the one who lent him her books and gave him suggestions for further reading.

Maybe it was those conversations that led him to start literacy classes in a shanty town. When he thought about Nati, it seemed to him that people who presented themselves as the only artists and creators were obsessive narcissists. To highlight their vapid self-images, they had to devalue the cultural practices of the people at large. They were obsessed with selling new spaces with the sole purpose of silencing debate. Their principal motivation, the search for money and acclaim, led them to fight for institutions in which to circulate their own ideas, instead of investing public resources in popular creative activities.

Many intellectuals see themselves as smarter than the rest, even if they pontificate about things they know nothing about. In the early 1970s, many of them were structuralists or, at least, had a high opinion of authors like Althusser, who was totally opposed to humanism, to any collective or popular attempt to transform society or change people's lives. *Reading Capital,* written by Althusser and Balibar, became more than a guide for reading *Capital,* it became a substitute for reading it. Many authors set themselves up as experts on Marx without ever having turned the pages of his books, simply basing their ideas on Althusser's book or on that of his student, Marta Harnecker.

Goyo could not make his own interpretation of Marx fit Althusser's. Structuralists attributed this difference to Goyo's humanism, to his closeness to common people. For them, directly participating like everyone else in popular movements was at odds with their scientific spirit. They looked down on the plain language Goyo used in speaking about important theories, because they themselves were forming an exclusive group by using vapid language that gave the impression of hiding theoretical baggage that ordinary people could never attain. They were like doctors who write illegible prescriptions so that people will credit them with unattainable knowledge.

People had taught Goyo not to pretend he knew about things he was ignorant of. Ever since he was a small child, he had loved reading, and he had come to understand that the exclusionary language used by the elite hid more mediocrity than creativity. He knows that many ordinary people are culturally more intelligent than intellectuals, himself included. Within the narrow concept of intelligence that some defend, he feels smarter than those who do not realize that they have a lot to learn from people like those attending La Verneda–Sant Martí center. He was always sure that the structuralists' put-downs were a product of their compulsive need to place them-

selves above the rest and of their nonchalance when it came to really reading the works they dared to pontificate about.

Goyo gave and coordinated seminars for members of the anti-Francoist
movement. Many of the speakers showed great readiness to talk about
books they had never read. On one crucial night, someone was conducting
a debate on *What Is to Be Done?* One young industrial worker criticized Lenin's work for its scorn of workers' democracy and its setting up of party
dictatorship. The speaker claimed this was erroneous, alleging that the Bol-
shevik leader had always defended a democratic stance, as could be seen
in *State and Revolution.*

As they left, Goyo asked the speaker where in *What Is to Be Done?* he had
seen a defense of workers' democracy. The response was shocking. The
speaker admitted that he had not had time to read the work, but that the
political point of the seminar was to make people understand the importance of Lenin's leadership. Goyo arrived home furious, imagining the
young worker reading a difficult book after a hard day's work, while the
intellectual silenced him without having even glanced at it. That night
Goyo made a vow that he still keeps: "I must do something to help end this
submissiveness." He immediately grabbed *Capital* and *Reading Capital.*
After staying up all night, he reached a conclusion: Althusser had not read
Capital.

No one believed him; it seemed an exaggeration even to enemies of the
creator of structuralist Marxism. It sounded like a disrespectful attack on a
distinguished intellectual. Some people even dismissed his rebellion
against official hierarchies of knowledge and in favor of egalitarian dialogue by arguing that it showed a lack of humility.

Goyo wanted debates to discuss the writings and talk about the relationship between different interpretations of the texts. However, the structuralist and poststructuralist media rejected this process; they did not need to
reason, discuss, or even read anything. Their interpretations were the most
interesting not because they were true but because they were theirs; thus
they were above good and evil, truth and falsehood.

Years later, in *The Future Lasts Forever,* Althusser confessed that he "knew
almost nothing about the history of philosophy and almost nothing about
Marx (I had of course studied earlier books about him, but the only thing
I had seriously read by him was volume one of *Capital*). . . . Raymond Aron
was not entirely wrong in speaking about 'imaginary Marxism' with reference to me and to Sartre."

How many millions of people are these kinds of authors deceiving? How many voices are silenced by them and their followers? The problem is not just in classrooms with authoritarian teachers; it is everywhere. Even in liberation movements there are leaders who want to feel superior to other people, and who look for prestige and money, constantly building new spaces for silence.

KAFKAESQUE REFLECTIONS

Goyo dislikes the ageist statement many "rockers" used in the 1960s: "Never believe a man over thirty." He instead uses another one: "Never believe an intellectual who looks down on popular knowledge." He believes in people like those who attend the literary circle. They talk about what they've read, their reflections and conversations. The young worker gave his opinion on *What Is to Be Done?* because he had read it; otherwise he would have listened and asked questions. He had thought about it in light of his experiences, desires, and observations. He understood that Lenin's work was as disconnected from his reality as it was from the egalitarian, democratic aims he was fighting for. But the speaker silenced him, claiming that his reading was dogmatic and erroneous. Such behavior kills people's motivation to read.

Juan was able to avoid that frustration, luckily. His daughter spent five years trying to persuade him to sign up at an adult education center. When he finally did, he started a process that turned him into a Kafka enthusiast and a promoter of self-reflection, in all senses of the word. His interest in Kafka's *Letter to His Father* was not coincidental. The group reads literature, not about literature. In the school system, information about authors and their works is frequently a required part of class. Sometimes it is so extensive as to replace the readings themselves. Often, students study Kafka without even reading *Metamorphosis* or any of his other works.

At the group meetings, people want to get past that perspective and to actually live literature. Personal readings must be free of the hypothetical or real intentions and circumstances of their authors. The group considers authors' personal histories, problems, and ideas as another narrative to bear in mind, rather than the real, required key to the text's meaning.

Juan emphasizes information about authors and their works. When he chooses a reading, he devours everything he can find about the book and its author. The group appreciates his input as information to keep in mind, without considering it indispensable for their interpretations.

Juan considered *Letter to His Father* a valuable discovery. On the one hand, it is literature, because it is accepted as such and because it is a story. On the other hand, it is a text about literature, because of the information it provides about the author and the circumstances that may have motivated him to write.

Juan is quite sure that there is a connection between Kafka's lack of communication with his father, narrated in *Letter to His Father*, and Gregor Samsa's situation with respect to his family, narrated in *Metamorphosis*. He reached his conclusion by reading both books, not by converting some critic's affirmations into absolute truths to be transmitted to the group. *Letter to His Father* is different from a historical or scientific work containing verifiable truths. It is, rather, Kafka's description of his own life, one of the many possible interpretations: his own.

Even more than *Letter to His Father*, Juan finds the words of a letter Kafka wrote to his girlfriend's father particularly meaningful: "I live with a family, among very good and affectionate people, more strange than a stranger. I hardly speak to any of them, because I have absolutely nothing to say to them. Anything that is not literature fills me with disgust and hate."

Juan has redefined his role and his thoughts in the group. He attends the gatherings, bringing his own readings of diverse texts, both from the agreed-upon books and from writings about the writers, their works, and their eras. In this way, he fulfills the role abandoned by the teacher and reclaimed by part of the group.

His ways of reading and being have evolved into a very self-reflexive process: he constantly thinks of his own history and the different interpretations made over time. Reflecting on the past calls into question the accuracy of the dichotomy Erikson had established as defining adulthood: integration or desperation. Juan is not desperate for his past; his position is closer to integration, since he feels satisfied with his life. But there is one big difference from Erikson's analysis. Juan's fullness is a result of his satisfaction with his overall journey. From a very intense present, he generates new stories about his past and projects for his future. The anti-ageist feeling of being in time for everything, even for reevaluating his past, recovering elements which until now went unnoticed, makes him want to make every instant of his present and future extraordinary.

He is grateful to Kafka for promoting self-reflection. *The Trial*'s author lived like an impenetrable intellectual; his solitude grew out of his inability to relate to his family and friends, in addition to his isolation in his job at an insurance company. Literature was the best way for him to live with himself. Some people think about success before writing and, as they fill pages, concentrate on whether their style or subject is appropriate for winning contests. The group thinks that Kafka's need to write was more profound; on his deathbed, he asked his friend Max Brod to destroy his writings. Maybe that is why, rather than winning prizes, his work has immortal value.

Juan is a popular intellectual of the sort Machado admired. His literary work is directly connected to people's existence and communication. Both Kafka and Juan reflect on their relationships with the people around them. The former does so with academic language, the latter with the preoccupations of the people.

That reflection led Kafka to write some of the most penetrating books of all time, and it leads Juan to engage in conversations that open new dimensions to people who participate in them. There are people like Kafka whom we will never get to know, and others like Juan whom history and official literature will ignore. Men and women who are either academic or popular intellectuals share one essential component: they create new possibilities for communication between people.

6

Rosalía

Dialogic Research

EXCLUSIONARY RESEARCH

Some members of the literary group formed part of a research team that studied participation and nonparticipation in adult education, a study that was carried out by the Research Center (CREA) at the Universitat de Barcelona. The people from La Verneda–Sant Martí center involved in the project had a clear social aim: to provide new educational opportunities for people who lacked them. They wanted to find out why people who had had scant educational opportunities in childhood tended not to participate in courses as adults, and they wanted to find out what changes needed to be made to bring about greater equality.

Laura, the research project coordinator, was very worried: many studies conclude that people with low academic levels are not motivated to participate. This finding justifies gearing courses towards people with high academic levels, giving more to those who already have more and thereby closing the circle of cultural inequality.

Rosalía, the most active member of the literary circle in the research team, was very upset when she found out about those studies. "That's all we need. As if we didn't have enough trouble with people who think they're so clever, now even those who carry out researches about people like us want to give us complexes." Though she had had few educational opportunities and sometimes thought she had no aptitude for schoolwork, Rosalía was always incredibly interested in learning. Of all the barriers that had impeded her participation, one was particularly painful: the way people who had greater opportunities looked down on her abilities and motivation. Tears welled up in her eyes as she recalled the reactions she had to endure at her sister's house when she dared to ask, "Who is Marx?" That was all that was needed to label her uncultured.

The group members asked why those studies had so much impact and whether they were well founded. Laura responded that their influence had less to do with their scientific basis than with their concordance with the elitist prejudices of people in high society and academic circles. Unfortunately, most researchers had organized the collection of their data without first reflecting on basic social theories. It was not unusual for those members of a research team who made the decisions to be unaware of fundamental works in the field. Nevertheless, their conclusions were those the rich and powerful expected to hear: that the underprivileged participate less than others because they do not want to, while cultured people show great motivation.

Rosalía was only willing to participate if this study was going to be different: "I won't work to sink those of us who need more encouragement." The research team was going to conduct a survey, and the first question was: "Over the past year, did you take any courses?" The coordinator explained that usually participation studies dismiss the negative answers, assuming that the answer "no" means that respondents are unmotivated.

The group thought that such a study might well lead to exclusionary conclusions. For example, that societies in the south participate less than those in the north because they are less motivated; or that within each country, people with low academic levels participate less because they lack motivation. Findings like these mean that victims—people or groups—are blamed for their own exclusion.

Rosalía took the questionnaire to groups from the La Verneda–Sant Martí center to be debated in the groups. She imagined a different kind of survey with a questionnaire beginning: "Have you read any classic works of literature in the past twelve months?" Only those who answered affirmatively would continue to be interviewed, on the assumption that the rest had no literary motivation. Everyone in the literary circle said that before attending it, they would have answered negatively. Actually, it would be unnecessary to spend money to find out what trends this type of study would show: northern countries value classics more than southern ones do; and within every society, those with superior academic levels are more motivated to read.

In such a study, conclusions about what action to take would differ, but all of them would carry exclusionary effects. One could label people from the north or people with high academic levels as potential participants in literary circles; this implies labeling people in the south as unmotivated to participate. Another exclusionary conclusion could be the need to extend motivation to read classic literature to southerners and people with low levels of academic training, that is, the creation of a program based on deficit theory that would assume these people and groups lacked motivation. Both would stem from an elitist assumption: those of us who provide and conduct research on education have motivation, while those who do not participate lack it.

These methods would never lead to the recruitment of a group of people like the subjects of this book. Their spectacular learning is grounded in their faith in their own abilities and motivation; thus it is impossible to classify them as people of low cultural levels just because they belong to sectors of low academic levels or resources. Without degrees or money, people can understand and enjoy great literature if they find a setting that encourages rather than destroys them.

AGAINST CONFINING PEOPLE IN CULTURAL LEVELS

What types of literature can people understand and enjoy according to their social and academic standing? People who are guided by the elitist point of view of dominant knowledge try to make it impossible for those with low levels of education to read Kafka, Dostoyevsky, or Joyce. What is worse, they discourage people's desires. Those who fight against confining people to fixed levels, while still participating in dominant cultural practices, consciously encourage people to read any kind of literature while unconsciously discouraging them from entering into the restricted knowledge of the elite.

This is what Goyo did when someone proposed that the group read Joyce's *Ulysses*. His spontaneous reaction revealed the exclusionary tendencies every intellectual harbors, even though he says he is in favor of complete equality: "Many people consider *Ulysses* the best modern novel ever written, but it's very complicated; more people buy it than read it." Some people heard these words as: "You haven't come that far, you are not cultured enough to read that book."

Luckily, Rosalía is a very rebellious woman, and she explained how the group members felt. Goyo was moved when he saw, reflected in the sincerity of his admired friend, the image of the worst side of himself. For days and nights, he searched for the roots of such an attitude in his own journey through Joyce's literature.

One Sunday long ago, he went to a children's matinee, thinking that the movie being shown was about the Ulysses family, a cartoon family he read about in the comics every week. But what he watched was Ulysses, the protagonist from *The Odyssey*. From the start, he disliked that character, so different from the one he had expected, and he became bored waiting for the second film to begin.

Years later, he would become an enthusiast of *The Odyssey*, which was more related to his dreams than the less humane *Iliad*. When he told stories to children, the ones they liked most were the ones he based on *The Odyssey*. He watched the movie again several times, finding it more interesting each time.

In college Goyo did not study Joyce or his books. On his first day in Barcelona, where he had gone in search of work and an apartment for himself and three friends, Clemente, the brother of someone Goyo had met on the train, took him from a boardinghouse on Escudellers Street to Clemente's own home. He offered the friends lodging and ended up acting as guardian to the four underage boys.

That same night, they sat at the living room table, and their host began reading aloud from a very strange text. Instead of listening, however, Goyo was wondering why Clemente had so generously and quickly offered his hospitality. Years later, Goyo was talking to Clemente about his enthusiasm for Joyce's *Ulysses*, until his ex-guardian exclaimed, "That is the book I read the night we met. What were you thinking about while I thought you were listening to me?"

After reading all of Joyce's works, Goyo still felt unable to do two things that really mattered to him: read *Ulysses* in English and understand *Finnegans Wake*, Joyce's last book. Even though Valverde's Spanish translation and Mallafré's Catalan version are both exceptional, *Ulysses'* puns on the evolution of English language, for example, are still untranslatable. *Finnegans*

Wake frustrated Goyo even more, as it is written in a linguistic mishmash he found impossible to understand.

It was not just a personal problem. At a Joyce conference, he found out that the problem extends to many people with college degrees. Even on a deserted beach on the Cíes Isles, an unknown literature professor passed by and offered his unsolicited "help": "You are starting a great book; few people manage to finish it." Throughout this barrage of memories, Goyo saw how his own failures led to his spontaneous exclusionary reaction to the proposal to read *Ulysses*. Somehow, what he said sounded like, "How are you going to understand it, if even we members of the elite have difficulties with it?"

The group did not wait for him to change his mind before taking action. On the contrary, their transformative reactions caused and consolidated his change. The first debate ended with no conclusion about the reading; those who wanted to would leaf through it and report their impressions to the group. Before Goyo realized it, some people were already devouring the book.

Just by chance, Rocío poured out her impressions of the work and Goyo discovered that, instead of leafing through it, she was about to finish it. At some points she sailed through the pages and at others she plunged deep into them. She said, "I really like it because it makes me reflect on things I had already thought about, but not really reflected on deeply."

In the debate, people contrasted Joyce's *Ulysses* with Homer's *Odyssey*. They valued the way the contemporary novel turned the everyday tales of Leopold Bloom, an average man, into art; this differed from the extraordinary deeds of the hero of *The Odyssey*. *Ulysses* is epic in expressing the thoughts and internal speech that go through the minds of everyone at all times.

In *The Odyssey*, the faithful wife, Penelope, waited ten years for Ulysses' return. In *Ulysses*, Molly Bloom is next to her husband in the bed where, earlier that same day, she has been with her lover. Her whirling feelings are reminiscent of prolonged insomnia and slow awakenings. Part of the group agrees that it is quite acceptable to omit periods or commas from the whole chapter, "because when we digress on a whim we don't use any periods or commas either." The others complain, "It's called creativity if a famous author does it and grammar mistakes when we do it."

Their comments surprised Goyo and corrected his mistake in having tried to curb the group's desire to tackle a difficult but very interesting reading. Luckily, their comments did not depend on him or on the projection of his own failures; the group has its own dynamic and it advances with or without his presence.

WE ARE NOT "CULTURAL DOPES"

Laura wonders how many exclusionary attitudes like Goyo's are to be found in studies about the motivation and abilities of people without college degrees. She also reflects on how much direct group participation, such as participation in the literary circle, is necessary to overcome the attitudes of an intellectual class that admires itself so much.

The research team involved very diverse people in the project, including college faculty from different departments and universities, professionals and adult education volunteers, participants and nonparticipants. The most retrograde technocrats considered this openness a sign of a lack of seriousness, while Rosalía thought it was only logical: "Could you imagine if they didn't let us participate in a study about our participation!"

Listening to the literary circle's participants talk about research and literature, Laura was as enthusiastic as Goyo. Their comments about participation and nonparticipation were different from those she had read and heard from people recognized as officially competent researchers.

The debates were as open as the team was diverse. Profound theorizing was mixed in with seemingly banal questions. Rosalía was in the midst of it all, since she had learned the most, and she made particularly novel contributions. She began to be reconciled with the scientific community when she read that Garfinkel, in *Studies in Ethnomethodology*, had written that people are not "cultural dopes." She did not read entire books on the theoretical basis for the study, but she worked, reflected, and debated various texts that the research team considered crucial. She heard the Garfinkel passage orally translated into Spanish by one of the researchers.

Althusser's name was engraved on her mind. After having dared to ask who Marx was, she had been called uncultured. Althusser, on the other hand, without having read Marx's work, had created a whole legion of followers who parroted his positions in order to better understand *Capital*. Her criticism reached its height when she found out that Althusser had strangled his wife. And now, at research team meetings, she was hearing that his reproduction theory denied social subjects the ability to reflect, converse, and transform their lives. Rosalía said it was the same old story: the elite who have had easy lives scorn ordinary people who struggle against inequality and treat them as if they are simpleminded.

Rosalía's educational participation and cognitive advances were inseparable from her opposition to petty intellectuals who called her ignorant. It did not shock her in the least to find people whose theories scorned the abilities and motivation of people like her. It made her sad and angry, but it was to be expected.

It was motivating to discover great literary authors like Machado and Lorca, who valued popular knowledge differently from those other, shoddy writers. But she attributed the egalitarian ways of people like Machado and Lorca to their idealism; they were executed or exiled as a reward for being common people.

The self-confidence she needed grew with the discovery that democracy, so feared by the elite, was reaching the scientific community. She was thrilled to find that the major authors in the social sciences were developing theories that showed faith in social subjects' abilities to reflect, converse, and transform. She enjoyed reading an interview with Giddens, in which he said, "Women have made the revolution of the century." She thought it was only normal that artists who were enraged by intellectual democracy would look to Nazi writers like Heidegger and his followers for inspiration. She liked hearing that Habermas had developed important critical theories attacking those ideas. She already knew, through the literary circle, that he had taken intersubjectivity as the basis for his theory of communicative action.

Rosalía was encouraged upon seeing that the most serious people had faith in the abilities of people like her. Years earlier she had thought that Paulo Freire was the only one. She was lucky enough to see Freire twice during his first stay in Barcelona. The first was at a popular lecture, held in a room packed with people from the neighborhood and from small towns, haphazardly mixed with college students and professors. The second was at the ceremony where he was awarded an honoris causa doctorate.

On one of these two occasions, the Brazilian teacher gave a theoretical talk on educational practices. On the other, he spoke of his love for Elza, the woman who was his companion from childhood until her death, and Nita, the woman he was living with at the time he gave the talk. Almost everyone would have expected him to give the theoretical talk at the academic function and his declaration of love at the popular function.

Paulo did just the opposite, inverting the categories of a society classified by cultural levels. It was easy to justify his choice to the academics: "I am not going to explain my works because you have already read them; otherwise, it would make no sense for me to be receiving an honorary doctorate." It sounded refreshingly human, in an auditorium that desperately needed to hear such sentiments.

At the popular event, the audience filled up every corner of the room, including the stage and stairs. One sign read: "Thanks to you, there are many of us." Freire was at a long table, surrounded by university representatives. Only one person, Núria, was not an academic; she was a participant in a literacy course. After she spoke, Paulo got up to hug her. This was the high point of the evening; the people who were there still recall the emotion of the applause. The literary circle members will always remember the ceremony at which the most important of all educational authors paid homage to people like her, to their abilities to learn and transform their lives.

COMMUNICATIVE GATHERINGS AS DIALOGIC RESEARCH

Should people participate in research about their own participation? Can a scientific concept be elaborated on the subject without taking into account the voices of these social subjects? Answering "yes" to the first question and "no" to the second led the research team to introduce some important transformations in their work.

The team's position was becoming more dialogical with every piece of research. In fact, their theory had always been critical and dialogical, but only part of their methodology was based on dialogue. At the time Rosalía joined the team, they still had not dared to change certain criteria imposed by the dominant scientific communities.

The literary circle was more dialogical than the university group. Dominant academic trends ignored the advances made by contributions such as Habermas's, and they opposed dialogic action. Equality of differences was absent from a process in which the weight arguments carried depended on who had put them forward. Most research teams decided what data to gather, interpreted their findings, and drew conclusions. The people who were researched only contributed one piece of information, and they did not even know how it was going to be interpreted. People like Rosalía felt used by that kind of action.

On traditional research teams, the arguments of academic power carried more weight than the power of arguments. Submission was assured: those with higher status would act later as judges of contests entered and exams taken by those still in lower positions. This subordination made dialogic rationality difficult to achieve, and sometimes meant that the best contributions were disregarded.

Often, the people researched did not know the aims of the project they were involved in; they were used like objects. Garfinkel did a study proposing a new tutorial system: he would only answer "yes" or "no" to students' questions. All students had to explain researchers' answers, without knowing that he was choosing his answers at random. Rosalía felt hurt that even this author would use people. Angrily, she said, "I would not like to come across any professor capable of using me like that, using my desire to learn so he could play science."

The literary group members were very critical, commenting on a book written by an expert on group discussion. They disliked the content as well as the presentation. The people researched were excluded from any contribution to the process: from any decision as to who would form part of the group, when and how they would meet, what they would talk about, and what would conclude. Garfinkel's concept of communication is totally opposed to Habermas's: "Communication is never transparent. It is modeled on war." Even the tone of the study seemed to show no respect for the people involved, for example, in its claim that "the group is born and dies when and where the preceptor wants."

Rosalía refused to participate in discussion groups like those proposed by that expert. However, she would agree to participate in discussions similar to those of the literary circle. Stimulated by her protests, the university research team reevaluated its methodologies, taking contributions from social theorists (Freire, Habermas, Mead, Schütz) and dialogic practices from popular projects like La Verneda–Sant Martí. Thus, this team developed a new qualitative technique grounded in the circle's dialogical approach: the social gatherings.

Through communicative gatherings, people researched by the team were given the opportunity to intervene with their reflections at any point in the process, including the analysis of information they had contributed and the decisions about their conclusions. The "methodologically relevant gap" Habermas saw, even in studies like Garfinkel's, was thus removed. Work meetings were based on egalitarian dialogue: the speaker's social standing was irrelevant; all that mattered were the arguments he or she contributed.

Free from the shackles of academic hierarchies, people like Rosalía have subversive potential that gives research great creativity and cause for reflection. The process is very beneficial to tenured professors. Once they see that their arguments will not be accepted without grounds, they have to make educational efforts to reason them out, rereading and going back to reflect on many issues. The language is dialogical; deceit or concealment is discarded. All parts of the study are available to whoever wants to consult them, and participants may contribute opinions that may even modify findings.

The results of the dialogic research were surprising. On the one hand, some things the team expected to find were confirmed: word of mouth is a good way of breaking down barriers to the participation of socially and culturally excluded sectors of society. A nonparticipant will come if someone else tells, insists, informs, and encourages him or her, sometimes even coming along to the classroom. On the other hand, some contributions disproved suppositions that were very deep rooted in many specialists. Goyo had spent years proclaiming that word of mouth was a great way to open possibilities to everyone. However, in the participation study, communicative gatherings pointed out important limitations to this, in terms of reaching sectors of society that have no means of communicating with participants who can express positive and motivational interest.

A wave of emotion went through the communicative gatherings, questioning why participation was concentrated in sectors with higher academic and social levels. There is social prestige in getting a master's degree, but discredit in signing up for literacy classes. There are always courses for qualified professionals, but it is hard for people with low-paid jobs to get training. Like Leopold Bloom, the group members have innumerable everyday thoughts that can contribute to knowledge about people like themselves. But those reflections do not seem to interest the mediocre elite members who call their activities "research," when in fact all they do is to reaffirm assumptions that are intended to keep their privileges far away from people they consider to be socially inferior.

7

Antonio

Gypsy Contribution to the Dialogue

TOURISTS CONSUMING GUITARISTS

Antonio played guitar at a place on the Costa Brava. It was hard for him to talk about his memories of his first night. Though his family had warned him about how he would be treated, he wanted to show everyone the magic he could make with his guitar strings. At first the audience seemed interested in his music, but a few minutes later they started to talk, and then to laugh, and finally to shout.

The most licentious tourists asked Antonio and his flamenco dancer to join them. One man lashed out at the dancer with his poisonous tongue. "You're my girlfriend." That sentence was the first of a barrage of lascivious claims. Though the girl managed to keep a smile frozen on her face, both she and Antonio felt the humiliation cut them to the quick. When they were finally alone again, their bodies spoke with sadness, but their mouths only formed words about their happiness at the success of their show.

Returning home, Antonio's sleepy mind opened his spirit to the image of the ring his whole family formed when singing authentic flamenco songs. A female child danced passionately in the center of the circle, protected by all the Gypsy women. No one would dare injure her purity; the women would have destroyed any outside aggressor. Suddenly, the peace was broken, the girl was in a place where drunken tourists sexually harassed her. She searched desperately for her people, but they were not there to protect her.

The literary group participants who were lucky enough to share words and songs with Antonio quickly overcame their prejudices about Gypsy violence and the impossibility of liberation for Gypsy women. The guitar accompanied songs describing violence against Gypsies and the attacks of the dominant white minority on other peoples and cultures.

Emran and Sengul, two girls of three and thirteen, washed car windshields at an intersection in Pisa. One day their eyes sparkled brightly: a driver had given them a doll! Seconds later Emran lost an eye and Sengul an arm, when the bomb inside the gift exploded. The assassin did not know them, he did not even want anything from them. All he knew was that they were Gypsies; all he cared about was that they had taken refuge in his city after fleeing the Balkan crisis. These motives were sufficient for him to mutilate them pitilessly. The mayor of Pisa justified the act as "defensive aggressiveness."

The non-Gypsy community said that these attacks were the work of killers and protested if anyone argued that they were acts of white violence. The situation is entirely different, though, when the victim is a non-Gypsy; suddenly everyone wants to talk about Gypsy violence. Antonio rejects both of these reactions; he says that we will only live in peace if we stop blaming entire groups for the violence of some of their members.

Emran and Sengul had escaped the war. Their families had bad memories of that kind of conflict. Half a century earlier, the Nazis had killed four thousand Romany people at once, shattering the heads of the smallest children against trees. The literary circle members had heard a lot about Gypsy aggression but not about aggression against Gypsies. They knew that the Holocaust had struck the Jewish community, but they were unaware that other groups, like Gypsies, had also been massacred.

Racist images of violence were thrown into disarray by the group's reading of *Romance de la Guardia Civil* (Civil Guard Ballad), by Lorca. In it, the Gypsy city awakens in danger because doors are opened everywhere. Shots are heard and "girls run hunted by their braids." The group had never reflected upon the fact that white society has armed institutions with which to protect itself and keep its laws from being broken, while Romany people face aggression from both non-Gypsies and Gypsies every day without that safeguard.

The flamenco dancer's feeling of helplessness was dramatically reflected in another poem in the *Gipsy Ballads* collection. Antoñito El Camborio feels so defenseless that he finds himself asking for the poet's help, asking him to call the Civil Guard instead of writing Antoñito's death without saving him from three bloody blows. In the same poem, Lorca calls Antoñito "a true gypsy, dying of starvation like so many others because he refused to sell his age-old voice to the high-class man who had only money, which is a small thing." Antonio did not sell his voice either; in order to "repay" him for his magic, you had to appreciate his music or, at least, respect him as a person. People at the night spots he frequented were familiar with the pilgrimage many artists made, playing music in the hope of having a true flamenco promoter hear them one night.

After Antonio went through another similar nightmare, a waiter recommended that he should forget about the tourists. "Don't think they treat you like that just because you're a Gypsy; they look down on anyone from the south because they think we are poor, underdeveloped, and stupid. But if they laugh at us, I laugh at them; we have to play the part they want so they give up their cash; but as people we are far above that trash; forget about them! Remember my advice: Just say, 'Yes, sir, okay, sir,' take the money, to hell with him and on to the next one."

For some time, on the outside Antonio played the part of the docile guitarist, while on the inside his Gypsy soul violently rejected all the human and artistic misery caused by that type of clientele. He also found audiences who appreciated his art and his person, people with whom he could have formed friendships in other contexts. But just a small group of troublemakers was all that was needed to ruin the whole atmosphere. At night he would go and play his guitar and sing authentic flamenco songs with his cousins in places where the customers were much more communicative. This took him away from the kind of tourism that consumes people.

LANDLESS PEOPLE

Antonio's participation in the literary circle led to different interpretations of every text. Poetry was never so alive as in the year of his attendance. Just as a stage is bathed in color when a flamenco dancer appears, the readings and discussions were colored by guitar music and songs of friendship.

The opened doors were one of the most commented-upon images. We *"payos"* close people out of our apartments and houses with security doors and dead bolts; we close people out of Europe with walls. The Romany nation has no country, and its people reject borders. In a non-Gypsy area, you can be robbed or even raped without a single one of your neighbors coming to your aid; their passivity may even make your suffering worse. In a Gypsy shanty town, everyone protects everyone else against the possibility of law-breaking.

Payos' history is full of wars waged to conquer or defend exclusive spaces. The group was surprised to learn that Gypsies reject the idea of fighting for their own country; their desire has always been to share all the land with other communities. They have mixed with people from different continents and yet they have maintained their identity, enriching it with a multitude of variants. They stand out for their cultures and relationships, instead of borders, states, armies, and flags.

Antonio avows that most people are peaceful and friendly, whether they are Gypsies or not. The nomadic tradition has given his people a special willingness to share spaces with different cultures, as well as to achieve creative miscegenation. The group read and discussed a talk given by García Lorca in which he said that the *cante jondo* (the "deep song" of flamenco singing) was created in Andalusia through the mixture of different cultures: the Gypsy culture, possibly from India; the Saracen culture from Arab countries; and the liturgical songs of the Spanish Church.

At the La Verneda–Sant Martí adult education center, Gypsies and non-Gypsies have spent time together for twenty years without any clash. However, in the area as a whole, there was in both groups a certain fear of the other, which created a climate of potential violence and lack of understanding on both sides. The literary group was sorry that the lack of more opportunities like the literary circle meant that other non-Gypsies from the neighborhood were unable to communicate so openly with people like Antonio.

ETHNOCENTRISM VERSUS DIVERSITY

Goyo was greatly influenced by his friendship with Antonio. He lived flamenco as never before during a performance by Camarón,[1] in the midst of an extended Gypsy family. The performance took place in the open air and the area was crowded with people. Goyo was moved by the people's fervor and the incredible emotion shown by entire families. He decided to enjoy the experience fully, without trying futilely to get Antonio to play the part of a white man, without himself attempting to act like a Gypsy. But how could they enjoy their friendship with each one maintaining his own identity? For three years they saw each other nearly every day. Until then, Goyo had been closed off, without knowing it, on the payo's side of Barcelona's nightlife.

Antonio reached adulthood without finishing school. Ever since he was a child he had been obliged to help out his family. This was a common situation among all his cousins; they worked as traveling salesmen or harvested grapes. The girls tended to leave school as soon as they entered adolescence, to take on their new roles as Gypsy women.

There were no Romany education centers or multicultural schools where his attributes were respected. The wrongly titled "Gypsy schools" had been payo schools with Gypsy students. None of the teachers, curricula, organization, or values were Gypsy. There was no attempt even to adapt the schedule and calendar; it was impossible to find classes held from November to July for those who were harvesting grapes until October. Instead of changing the educational offering so that everyone could have an equal learning opportunity, the system tagged members of different groups as "unmotivated."

At school, Antonio experienced a strange world that had little to do with his family. The learning was unrelated to his culture. Everything seemed to point to the need to choose between two options: trying to succeed by giving up his Gypsy status or keeping his family ties by rebelling against the teaching he received.

The educational system took for granted that the Gypsy student body was difficult. Gypsy students got worse grades than others and had worse attendance, more lateness, and more indiscipline. Antonio began to wonder what the problem was: the school or his people. Was it his people's fault for taking young people to harvest grapes? What choice did they have? That work was a vital means of survival. Why did the system classify those students as "behind" instead of looking for ways to help them recover from their absence?

It is normally accepted that school absenteeism leads to an uncultured state and is caused by a family's lack of motivation. But Enrique Morente, the current king of flamenco, who left school at the age of eight, sings poems by Lorca, San Juan de la Cruz, Ibn Hazd, and Machado, among others, and puts *The House of Bernarda Alba, Don Quixote,* and *Oedipus Rex* to music.

At La Mina adult education center, Antonio found a project that was open to differences. Though it was also a payo institution, all the people there could have their own space in which to learn and relate to each other, since their knowledge was valued by everyone else. There he gained his basic school diploma, as well as the respect of non-Gypsies.

A Gypsy gang came in several times and defecated in the middle of the classroom. Antonio spoke with them, understanding their reasons for detesting all centers of education. He said that, although the school was not Gypsy, many Gypsies were benefiting from the teaching there and were appreciated as much as anyone else in the place; there were no more incidents. No payo teacher could have achieved that.

Listening to Antonio, the literary gathering spontaneously began to search for better learning opportunities for all groups. Some people supported the refusal of the educational system to accept Gypsy schools or Arab schools in the attempt to avoid excluding students from these groups and to facilitate their integration. Others questioned this stance, asking why, then, French, German, or North American schools were accepted. In general, people agreed that there was an ethnocentric prejudice discriminating between cultures from the north and those from the south.

Some people defended the idea of Gypsy schools based on Gypsy culture, just as payo schools were based on payo culture. Others proposed multicultural schools where all the cultures making up the student body could coexist equally. But they all rejected the ethnocentric attempt of the school system to impose one homogenic model on everyone: that of white, Western, male culture. On the contrary, the group suggested other educational contexts in which it would be possible to advance towards solidarity and equality.

RELATIVISM VERSUS EQUALITY

Antonio defended the idea that everyone had the right to learn whatever was necessary to avoid social exclusion. Any alternative should ensure the possibility of the entire student body acquiring a universal culture. Whether German or Gypsy, a school should include universal culture, seen from the German or Gypsy point of view, instead of reducing the curriculum to a few aspects of their respective group identities.

In the 1980s, relativism had become professionally and intellectually fashionable, even with professors. Some authors even attacked the right to literacy, arguing that it was a Western imposition on oral cultures. Antonio was angered by such opinions, because he and his family still suffer educational exclusion. He said that it is unfair for someone with a college degree and a steady job to discuss whether or not it is good for other people to be able to attain literacy.

He had never seen his people question educational opportunities. But he criticized the fact that schools gave only payo education. He said he was thoroughly tired of professionals who lived off educational institutions and attacked the small chance that socially excluded people had of gaining access to them. The Romany people are not relativist, but universalist. Enrique Morente, the famous flamenco singer, says, "Music cannot be racist. Good art must be universal."

The fashion for relativism led people in the circle to talk a lot about this perspective. Some read texts on the topic. At first they thought that the aim was to criticize Western ways and defend other people, but then they realized that this mode of thinking was a Western creation. That realization corresponded with Antonio's complaint. Relativist authors put into the mouths of excluded groups words that they do not dare say themselves: they oppose giving others the same educational opportunities that they themselves have had.

When excluded groups have a voice, they demand equal rights. One day Rosario, a representative of the only female Gypsy association in Catalonia, gave a talk at the university. She made it clear that she and her associates were proud to be Gypsies and women, and they wanted an education that was not bound by the limitations of payo institutions and the sexism of some Gypsies.

As was to be expected, the relativist position was expressed by someone who had enjoyed the boundless educational opportunities that Gypsy women sought; one college student told her, "That will make you lose your identity." Rosario admitted that some Gypsies acted like non-Gypsies when they studied, but emphasized that others focused their new knowledge from a Gypsy perspective. She pointed out that in all communities, not just hers, women have had to struggle for equal rights. She maintained that the best way to keep Gypsy women's identity in today's world was to reinforce it by ensuring that there were women lawyers, doctors, and teachers from the Romany people.

Rosario teaches other Gypsy women. She does it much better than the official teachers, but her lack of a college degree means that she cannot be given a contract. College entrance exams are made for non-Gypsies. At the same universities where Gypsies fail these exams, some professors try to "liberate" Gypsy students from the loss of identity their admission will allegedly entail. Gypsy women, on the other hand, fight for their right to education as people and as Gypsies.

GYPSY REBELLION AGAINST ETHNOCENTRISM AND RELATIVISM

Javier, a friend of Goyo's, once dared to bring up the subject of Gypsies before a payo audience. He felt sure of his knowledge and experiences, until one young woman sang a different tune. Her words expressed very personal sentiments, analyzed with penetrating intelligence. Her face lit up when she said, "I know what I'm talking about." When the talk ended, Javier and the young woman, Carmen, spoke about their Gypsy identity until Alberto, a payo man, came to pick her up.

Months later, Carmen was recounting her personal history on a trip to Valencia, her father's birthplace. From her tears, Javier could see how hard it was for a woman to confront ethnocentric and relativist postures. She became very sad, thinking of her female cousins. Many of them would leave school as preteens in order to dedicate themselves to family matters and stay "pure" for the future husbands. "Many Gypsies, like many non-Gypsies, are chauvinists and want us to be subordinate."

Ethnocentrism, by law, forces Gypsies to attend payo schools, with payo teachers and both payo and Gypsy students. It keeps the students and their families from participating in decisions about their learning conditions. The only way to reject this imposition is through absenteeism. Relativism applauds a refusal to participate in academic institutions in the name of a Gypsy identity that supposedly opposes any institution awarding educational diplomas or degrees that help remove social exclusion. Both relativism and ethnocentrism deny the educational rights of Gypsy girls: relativism by questioning these rights, and ethnocentrism by making what Gypsies see as unacceptable demands on Gypsy girls who want to exercise their rights.

Some Gypsy men want to keep their privileges over women and call those who demand equal rights "payos." One of Carmen's cousins had to pass the "handkerchief test" on her wedding day: some older women took her to a room where the *ajuntadora* inserted the white silk. Everything turned out well in the end, because it came out the right color; otherwise, the young woman and her family would have been in serious trouble, unless the groom said, "It was me." Carmen says that, luckily, this obligation is now disappearing. "We will reach a point where only those who truly want to will go through that, no one will be forced. We are transforming our culture and we have a right to do so, just as payos do. There are more and more Gypsy women who want to study. I find it incredible that there are intellectuals who want to make us fight against this basic right. The relativist stance only favors chauvinist gypsies and payos who are afraid of Gypsy women's societal advances. Such relativism is as harmful to the Gypsy community as it is to women overall."

Between their first conversation and their trip to Valencia, Carmen and Javier developed an intense relationship. Carmen's libertarian attitude was very uncommon in a non-Gypsy world that accused other cultures of chauvinism. Javier felt seduced by her bewitching looks, which persistently filled his mind. Sometimes their sincere friendship and collaboration was accompanied by fantasies of passionate love. Wishing to avoid problems, Javier restrained his desire for further encounters.

When they saw each other again, Javier neither explained nor hid his attraction. Carmen communicated intimate feelings with her words and with her body. Javier contained his desire to caress her physically, though he could not refrain from caressing her with his eyes and his voice. When they said goodbye, Carmen said, "I thought we were going to spend the night together." This was not a clichéd repetition of a seduction but a search for her true feelings. Kisses and caresses were the natural result of their sincere emotions, with no rules imposed from outside, no fears inside. The line between tender looks and sexual excitation disappeared; both sprang forth from their shared passion. No dominant culture accepts such self-determination in women.

Carmen and Alberto loved and desired each other so intensely that they had the utmost respect for each other's independence. Although a third person was now involved, Alberto helped his girlfriend by showing her the sincerity of his egalitarian feelings. He and Carmen used to go out with three other couples. These other couples found it strange that the only Gypsy in the group defended such a libertarian idea. She was breaking the stereotypical mold: Gypsy culture is retrograde, payo culture is liberal. When they spoke about the topic, Miguel and his girlfriend harshly criticized what they considered infidelity. But one day at Miguel's house, Carmen said she had arranged to meet Javier. Miguel accompanied her to the door and left her rigid with his offensive question, "When is it going to be my turn?"

Miguel's attitude annoyed her intensely. "That just shows you a payo's hypocrisy. Alberto and I are faithful to our love. Miguel is not faithful to his girlfriend, nor to his colleague, nor to me, if he considered me a friend until now. In his mind, there are only two kinds of women, one to be shut in the kitchen and the other to be treated like sluts."

Javier thought about that infuriating hypocrisy. Many payos who attack the Romany community for being chauvinist or for restricting educational rights for women refuse to let their own girlfriends go to classes or conferences that require a night away from home. Many careers are truncated because boyfriends and husbands protest if they hear talk about scholarships to study abroad.

Carmen, who is a Gypsy, married Alberto, who is a payo. Their love is greater than either community understands. Maybe the critical spirit brought on by their intermarriage has opened possibilities that hypocritical moralists like Miguel neither understand nor respect. Javier's feelings for Carmen continue despite their distance from each other. His memory of her tears on the trip to Valencia encourages him to continue the struggle for equal rights for all people from all cultures.

DIALOGUE AS EQUALITY OF DIFFERENCES

In the literary circle, Antonio found a communicative way of sharing differences. The Romany identity was a priority in his dialogue. Words and looks shed light where lack of comprehension had reigned. The wisdom possessed by Antonio's family, who were so often called illiterate, was seen to be as valuable as academic knowledge. Cultures are different, not superior and inferior; they are equal, not homogeneous.

The discussions revealed Antonio's capacities and shed light on the problems of relativism and ethnocentrism. The poor grades received by Gypsy students could be seen as a result of ethnocentric education, instead of ethnic inferiority. The aim was not to integrate the Romany community into the lowest positions of payo society, but to base social relationships and systems on collaboration and respect between different cultures. Antonio's active participation gave a Gypsy dimension to the group's literary interpretations.

In her talk, Rosario explained how girls were taught. "When they turn eighteen, they already have two kids, and as Gypsy women we do not like to leave children in day-care centers; that is an aberration to us." One college student was pleased to finally find an expression of relativism, a rejection of the official educational system. But Rosario continued, "They bring their children to the center; we put them in another room where a woman, who is very good, takes care of them." Immediately, she began to defend the right of Gypsies to participate in the educational system without losing their identity. That is, they considered a payo nursery school an aberration, but they organized a Romany nursery school.

Antonio enjoyed learning and teaching in the literary circle. Goyo would say that it was simultaneously both a Gypsy and a payo class. In that communicative space, people experienced a dialogue that approached the equality of differences. Antonio could keep and develop his Romany identity, other people could keep and develop their payo identities. At the same time, the whole group agreed on some common norms to make it work.

Manuel protested. "What about me? I don't see myself as a Gypsy or a payo. I am obviously Andalusian, but there is also a little Gypsy in me, and that's how I felt when I lived with them in the La Perona shanty town. Now, with the kids and grandkids I have, I am also a little Catalonian."

Little by little, each person begins to feel different and, at the same time, shares much with the others. It is not hard to agree on some norms to make dialogue possible. Everyone discusses one part of the text. Those who have spoken less than others in any given session have priority. The next books to be read are also chosen by consensus.

Some ethnocentrists criticize the literary circle because it gives the opinions of uneducated people the same consideration as the opinions of renowned authors. Ethnocentrists fear a loss of hierarchy in the educational system. It is not true, however, that all contributions are valued equally; it depends on their arguments. Nor are all attitudes given equal value. For example, participants reject the idea of one person trying to impose his or her opinion on the rest. Goyo knows that the educational system would be massively transformed if it were based on this dynamic; it would become more fair and open-minded.

Some relativists say that dialogue is an ethnocentric imposition on other cultures. They do not believe this democratic experience is superior to authoritarian educational projects. Antonio and the rest of the group, on the other hand, are in favor of democratic practices and against authoritarianism. They know that their dialogue differs from traditional uniformity.

Goyo says that this dynamic is dialogical. It establishes an equality of differences that opens the way for developing new identities. These, then, are the fruit of freely combining characteristics from one's own culture with admixtures from other communities. Gypsies feel that their identities are thereby reinforced and enriched.

PROFOUND FRIENDSHIPS IN SELF-INTERESTED SOCIETIES

Antonio left the group and stopped going out with Goyo at night when he began his own family. Belén soon had a daughter whose green eyes filled even the most desperate circumstances with hope. The last time Antonio and Goyo saw each other was at a Camarón concert.

Eleven years later, Goyo gave a talk at a penitentiary center. As he was getting ready to leave, a sewing teacher came up to him and said, "There's an inmate here who says he's a friend of yours; his name is Antonio Mejías." Goyo was heartbroken to hear that Antonio's sentence was a long one, for a crime against "public health." Antonio had already been in prison for nineteen months. Goyo's obsession with getting him out took up every moment until he was able to give his friend a hug.

At night, he remembered the times they had shared in places where people took and dealt drugs. They had been the only ones who did not share in any of the drug-taking. In his neighborhood, Antonio represented those who opposed the activities that were destroying Gypsies' communities, their traditional patriarchies and their new associations. Sometimes Goyo had feared a raid. It would have been hard to prove his innocence. He had also been in high-class establishments where people passed around cocaine. But there, people breathed with an air of immunity that allowed them to "do a few lines" without worrying too much about hiding. He was sure Antonio was innocent, but he also admitted the possibility of being wrong. He had always thought that social circumstances could lead people to do anything. What had happened to Antonio and his family?

When Goyo had moved from La Mina adult education center to La Verneda–Sant Martí center, Antonio had gone with him, helped him organize the literary circle, and livened up parties. Belén wanted to do what she could to make headway in another direction. She and Antonio tried to take over the cafeteria in the community center, but it was given to the wife of a policeman who worked there. The couple decided to open a bar close by, and the group helped them round up customers.

It was the worst time to start something like that. There was a campaign to try to get rid of shanties, and some people used the demonstrations as an excuse to attack the Gypsy families who lived in them. Times were hard for the neighborhood organizations that tried desperately to pacify the situation. Antonio and Belén went back to La Mina and to the family business. Had times been so hard that they'd become involved in shady dealings? If so, they must have changed a lot.

It only took a second to see in Antonio's eyes that he had not changed. After the joy of the embrace, Antonio was choked with emotion: "You know there could never be lies between you and me." He said he had been walking down the street with his daughter when Pedro, his neighbor, had gone by in his pick-up truck and asked Antonio to go and have a drink with him. In the bar, Pedro had said that before going home he had to pick up some watches from an apartment. Antonio became suspicious, but he kept quiet until he saw what was really going on.

They left the apartment arguing and angry. Antonio was upset that Pedro had betrayed him and furious at having put his daughter in danger. It was always the same; he trusted everyone and then, by the time he realized he was wrong, it was too late. Why was Pedro doing this to him? What did Pedro take him for? And what about Antonio himself? How had he been so stupid as to put his daughter at risk? He would do anything for her, and yet he'd put her in this situation. He had to get her out of there, in whatever way was possible.

The police showed up, shouting and running, protecting themselves behind the guns they aimed at the bungling apprentice trafficker and his two human shields. Antonio was wild with rage at seeing his daughter scared, with a gun pointing at her, and being frisked violently. He acted like an authentic Gypsy father, without thinking of himself, only of getting his little girl out of that terrible situation. He intervened with the police. In his spontaneous reaction, years, decades, centuries of indignation exploded. He had learned as a child that he had to defend his family using Gypsy ways, that he should mistrust a payo community that blamed his people for being

Gypsies. It was not the smartest reaction, but the one that could be expected after seeing his daughter in this situation.

Everything had already been decided. As the lawyer said at Antonio's trial, it was not a crime; it was a situation provoked by the police. Pedro repeated that the two bags were his and that he had involved Antonio and his daughter as a cover. When asked if he had anything to add, Pedro gave a moving speech, asking them not to convict his neighbor unjustly. There was no compassion, no truthful testimony, no justice. Several white policemen gave statements against Antonio, and his only defense was a Gypsy minor, related to the accused. The judge had him convicted before the trial even started; the judge spent the trial doodling. Goyo would have helped his friend no matter what, but Antonio's innocence made him even more determined to help.

He had always felt that there was little to be gained by going after small-time traffickers and much damage done by acting on racist prejudices that put innocent people in prison. To put an end to the harm done to groups and individuals by drugs, he believed, you have to go after the big Mafiosi and stop money laundering.

Goyo's friends gave the problem their all. The involvement of the payo community changed the situation. Suddenly, people around Antonio began to believe him. Until then, everyone had liked him, but not enough to eliminate their mistrust, since "you know, they all say they are innocent." Goyo explained that he had already experienced a similar case, while Franco was in power. During the struggle for democracy, Koldo went on a demonstration on the Ramblas, to protest the execution by garrote of Puig Antich. Someone threw a Molotov cocktail, everyone took off running, and Koldo was arrested. The police testified that he had been the aggressor, and the prosecutor asked for a twelve-year sentence. Due to the political moment, Koldo ended up serving just one year; he was, therefore, able to reincorporate himself into normal life. He became an adult education teacher.

On March 13, at 7:00 A.M., Antonio was released. He spent the whole day working on the entrance exam to the university for over-twenty-fives. The next day he had to go to a sewing shop where they wanted to offer him a contract. But first there was going to be a party that night. Just one sentence from Antonio's uncle from Zaragoza made Goyo laugh after arriving tired and late, with his briefcase: "Watch it, don't leave your bag lying around, there are a lot of Gypsies here," said Antonio's uncle.

The rhythm of the music brought together the youthfulness of a mother who had been pregnant nine times, the magic of the young guitarists, the incredible movements of four-year-old children, the dancing of a great-grandmother about to turn ninety, and the playfulness of her teenage granddaughters. As he watched, an attractive Gypsy girl sang lines from García Lorca's poetry. Goyo lost himself in a whirlwind of memories and projects. He had spent twenty years learning to read and live, from people like Manuel, Lola, Chelo, Rocío, Juan, Rosalía, and Antonio. Authentic cultural creation far surpassed classrooms and intellectual talks after dinner. He conjured up images of books related to the feelings, desires, and dreams of health workers, "housewives," retired people, construction workers, immigrants, dressmakers, and traveling salesmen. That would be good for people . . . and for literature.

NOTE

1. Camarón is usually considered to be the best flamenco singer of all times.

Index

Abilities, 7, 33, 48–49, 62, 104–105, 108–109; of adults, 51, 86; cognitive, 8; communicative, 7; learning, 40, 81

Action, 9, 13, 15, 21, 23, 35, 37, 39, 59, 62, 74–75, 86–87, 96, 105, 107, 111; communicative, 3–7; dialogic, 45, 59, 110; dramaturgical, 3, 5–7; normatively regulated, 3, 5–7; pedagogical, 13; political, 13; teleological, 3, 5–7; transformative, 19

Adorno, Theodor W., 2

Adult, 2, 8, 32, 47, 49, 50–51, 55–56, 63, 81, 83, 86–88; adulthood, 8, 16, 50, 63, 84, 100, 117; education, 21, 49, 54, 56, 67, 71, 81, 83, 85, 87, 92, 103, 108; education center, 6, 11, 21, 37, 39, 47–48, 80, 85, 99, 116, 118, 125–126; learning, 87–89; programs, 54; *See also* Participant

Ageism, 8–9, 12, 79–82, 85, 87, 89

Ageist 8, 12, 81, 99; barriers, 81; conception, 82; concepts, 8, 16, 86–87; discrimination, 9, 14, 24; education, 81

Altamira, Rafael, 49

Althusser, Louis, 12–13, 19, 97–98, 108; Althusserian Marxism, 13

Andalusia, 31, 116

An Andalusian Dog. See Un perro Andaluz

Animal Farm, 95

Antigone, 75

Apple, Michael W., 12

Aranguren, José Luis, 85

Aron, Raymond, 98

Austin, John L., 4

Bakunin, Mikhail A., 50

Balibar, Étienne, 97

Ballad, 11, 51, 92

Balzac, Honoré, 43

Barcelona, 32, 53, 67, 80, 85, 95, 103, 106, 109, 117

Barriers, 9–10, 21, 41, 45, 80, 104, 112; ageist, 81; antidialogical, 62; and communication, 48, 95–96; cultural, 9, 11, 33, 47, 62; elitist, 44; personal, 9, 12, 47–48; social, 9, 11, 47–48, 62

Baudelaire, Charles, 57

Beck, Ulrich, 2

Bello, Andrés, 41

Bernstein, Basil B., 12

Bilbao, 96

Bill of Rights for Participants, 54
Blasco Ibáñez, Vicente, 84
Blood Wedding, 55, 60
Bloom, 16
Bono, 106
Borges, Jorge Luis, 42, 44
Bourdieu, Pierre, 12
Bowles, Samuel, 12
Buñuel, Luis, 66, 68, 84

Calderón de la Barca, Pedro, 49
Camarón (José Monge Cruz), 116, 124
Cante Jondo, 116
Capital, 97–98, 108
Capitalism, 40, 43
Capitalist, 36–38, 40, 42, 62
Carpentier, Alejo, 34–35
Center for Social and Educational Research. *See* CREA
Cervantes, Miguel de, 42, 44, 58, 84
Civil Guard Ballad. *See Romance de la Guardia Civil*
Civil War, 33; Spanish, 47–48, 67, 75
Classist, 9
Communicative Action Theory, 2–3, 16, 20, 109
Communicative gatherings, 110–112
Community, 4, 12, 21, 25, 92, 95, 160; assemblies, 39; Gypsy, 121; Jewish, 114; non-Gypsy, 114; payo, 125–126; Romany, 122–123; scientific, 50, 108–109
Consent, 58
Constructivism, 23
Cortázar, Julio, 57
CREA, 6, 20, 87
Creating meaning, 1, 62; means of, 18
Creativity, 10; dialogic, 10–11; popular, 96
Crime and Punishment, 17
Cultural Intelligence, 1, 6–10, 49, 51, 61, 81, 87

Cultural Dope, 108
Culture, 8, 11–12, 42, 45, 53, 57, 62, 79, 85, 96; associations, 49, 59; barriers, 9, 11, 33, 47, 62; creation, 15, 127; communication, 45, 48, 58–59, 62, 85; dialogue, 45; equality, 55; inequalities, 31, 67, 103; levels, 105, 110; practices, 97, 105; transference, 10; wall, 48, 53

Dalí, Salvador, 31, 32, 60, 84
Deep Song. *See* Cante Jondo
Derrida, Jacques, 20
Dialogic, 5, 16–17, 51, 61, 110–11, 124; action, 45, 59, 110; creativity, 10–11; language, 57, 112; perspective, 7, 23–24; rationality, 54–56, 111; research, 22, 103, 110–112
Dissent, 58–59
The Divine Comedy, 49
Don Quixote, 10, 42, 44, 58–59, 89, 118
Dostoyevsky, Feodor, 105
Dramaturgical action. *See* Action
Durkheim, Émile, 3

Educational reforms, 22, 86
Egalitarian: dialogue, 1,2, 4, 6, 8–14, 18, 21–22, 25, 84, 98, 112; transformations, 13, 20
Elouard, Paul, 32
El siglo de las luces. See Explosion in a Cathedral
Equality of differences, 1, 22, 25, 73, 110, 122–124; feminism of, 74
Erikson, Erik H., 100
Ethnocentrism, 116, 120, 123
Exclusion, 6, 11, 15, 19, 22, 34, 37, 38, 42, 45, 74, 79, 81–84, 89, 104, 118, 120; educational, 15, 83, 119
Explosion in a Cathedral, 34, 36

Feminism, 14, 62, 74, 76, 80
Fictions, 42
Finnegans Wake, 106–107
Flamenco, 33, 113, 115–117
Flaubert, Gustave, 43
Foucault, Michel, 20, 70
Franco, Francisco, 42, 126
Francoist Women's Section, 80
Free Institution of Education, 72, 83–84
Freire, Paulo, 2, 8, 12–13, 20–21, 23, 44, 59, 61, 110–111
Freud, Sigmund, 20
Fuenteovejuna, 87, 89
The Future Lasts Forever, 12, 98

Gadamer, Hans-Georg, 4
Gades, Antonio, 89
García Lorca, Federico, 10, 31, 47–48, 51, 55, 58, 60, 62, 84, 114, 117, 127
García Márquez, Gabriel, 52–53
Garfinkel, Harold, 4, 108, 111–112
Germinal, 38, 42
Giddens, Anthony, 2, 13, 109
Gintis, Herbert, 12
Giroux, Henry A., 2, 12–13, 62
Goffman, Erving, 3
Granjas Revolution, 19, 43, 96–95
Guernica, 66
Gypsy, 25, 58, 83, 113–127; associations, 22, 119, 124; culture, 118, 122; schools, 117–118; women, 119–123, 127
Gypsy Ballads, 11, 31, 58, 66, 115

Habermas, Jürgen, 2–4, 11, 13, 15–16, 20, 51, 53–54, 71, 109–112
Harnecker, Marta, 97
Hazd, Ibn, 117
Heidegger, Martin, 20, 109
Hermeneutics, 4
Hernández, Miguel, 4, 33–34, 42

Historias de cronopios y famas, 41–42
Hopscotch, 41
The House of Bernarda Alba, 10, 60, 75, 118
Hugo, Victor, 42
Human Agency, 13

The Iliad, 106
Inequality, 2, 7, 20, 22, 25, 31, 39, 45, 68, 70, 109; cultural, 31, 67, 103
Information society, 19, 38, 45, 86
Institución Libre de Enseñanza, 72
Instrumental dimension, 1, 15; knowledge, 16; learning, 16–17, 60–61
Intelligence, 8, 50–51, 120; academic, 6–7, 51; adult, 50; concept of, 97; crystallized, 6; cultural, 1, 6–10, 49, 51, 61, 81, 87; fluid, 6; practical, 6–7, 51, 87
Interactive self-confidence, 10

Joyce, James, 16, 21, 54, 105–107
Juan de Mairena, 83–84

Kafka, Franz, 18–19, 91–94, 99, 100–101

La Barraca, 59, 85
La Mina, 118, 124–125
Language games, 4
La Regenta, 17
La Verneda-Sant Martí, 15, 41, 48, 50, 54–56, 60, 74, 80–83, 85, 87–89, 97, 103–104, 111, 116, 125
Lazarillo de Tormes, 39, 46
Learning, 2, 4–5, 8, 10–11, 16, 23–24, 41–42, 55, 61, 80–83, 86–87; concepts of, 3; dialogic, 1–3, 6, 12, 14–18, 20–24, 60–61; emancipatory, 62; instrumental, 15–17, 60–61; meaningful, 22–24; principles of, 1
Lenin, Vladimir Ilyich, 98–99

Les Misérables, 42
Letter to His Father, 99–100
Lifeworld, 13
Literary circle, 1–5, 10, 15, 18–21, 24–25, 32, 34, 41, 44, 47, 51, 53, 55, 57, 62–63, 75, 82, 85, 93, 96, 103–104, 108, 110–111, 114–116, 122–123, 125
Luckmann, Thomas, 23
Lyotard, Jean-François, 20

Macedo, Donaldo, 12
Machado, Antonio, 79, 83–85, 101, 109, 117
Mallafré, Joaquim, 106
Marx, Karl, 13, 21, 97–98, 104, 108
Marxism, 13, 98
Mead, George Herbert, 4, 17, 111
Metamorphosis, 91, 93–94, 99–100
Methodologically relevant gap, 111–112
Miss Sarajevo, 77
Morente, Enrique, 117, 119

Nanas de la cebolla, 34
Napoleon, 43
Nazi, 20, 109, 114; Neo-Nazi movements, 20
Nietzsche, Friedrich Wilhelm, 58
Nietzschianism, 20
Non-participants, 103, 108, 112
Normatively regulated action. *See* Action

Objectivism, 23
The Odyssey, 49, 75, 106–107
Oedipus Rex, 118
One Hundred Years of Solitude, 52
Onion Lullaby, 34, 42. *See also Nanas de la cebolla*
Orlandi, Cecilia, 76
Orwell, George, 95

Pàmies, Teresa, 85
Papá Goriot, 43–44
Parsons, Talcott, 3
Participant, 3, 5, 10, 18–19, 25, 40, 42, 44–45, 48, 51, 54–57, 60–62, 65, 68–69, 75, 80, 83, 85, 88–89, 91–93, 105, 108, 112, 114
Participation, 11, 14, 21, 45, 89, 95–96, 103–104, 108–110, 112, 115, 123
Pavarotti, Luciano, 77
Payos, 116–126. *See also* Romany
Penelope, 74–76, 107
Pérez Galdós, Benito, 66, 68
Piaget, Jean, 2, 8, 82
Picasso, Pablo Ruíz, 33, 66, 84
Pierre Menard, Author of the Quixote, 42–43
Postmodernism, 13, 20
Proust, Marcel, 57

Racist, 9, 11–12, 14, 21, 24, 114, 119, 126
Rape, 15, 20, 70, 73, 77, 116
Reading Capital, 97–98
Relativism, 24–25, 37, 118–120, 123
Research, 6, 8, 21, 23, 50, 83–84, 87, 103–105, 108, 110–112; dialogic, 22, 103, 110–112; exclusionary, 21, 103
Revolución de las granjas. *See* Granja's Revolution
Roig, Montserrat, 70
Romance de la Guardia Civil, 114
Romancero gitano. See Gypsy Ballads
Romances. *See* Ballad
Romance Sonámbulo, 58
Romany, 114, 116–117, 119, 120, 123; community, 122–123; identity, 122–123
Rosales, Luis, 60

San Juan de la Cruz, 117
Sappho, 14, 71–76

Sartre, Jean Paul, 98
Schaie, K. Warner, 8
Schütz, Alfred, 23, 111
Scribner, Sylvia, 8, 87
Sección Femenina. *See* Francoist Women's Section
Self-interested societies, 124
Sexism, 9, 39, 65–66, 70, 79–80, 119
Sexist, 14, 24, 65, 72, 74, 80
Skinner, Burrhus Frederic, 20
Solidarity, 1, 15, 18–22, 25, 36–38, 40, 44, 54, 67–68, 70, 87–88, 93, 95; conceptions of, 20
Somnambulist Ballad. *See Romance Sonámbulo*
Spaces for conversation, 18, 94
Spaces for silence, 18, 96, 99
Speech-act theory, 4
Stalin, Joseph, 44
Stalinism, 43–44
State and Revolution, 98
Sternberg, Robert J., 6, 17
Structure, 13, 19, 35, 62, 94, 96
Studies in Ethnometodology, 6, 108
System, 9, 13, 17–19, 40, 50, 62, 84–85, 92, 95, 99, 111, 117–118, 123–124

Teleological action. *See* Action
Tertulia, 1, 4, 57; *See also* Literary circle

Transformation, 1, 10, 12–15, 20, 33, 36, 40, 45, 55, 57, 62, 65, 67, 70, 72, 95, 110
The Trial, 94, 95, 100
Tristana, 14, 65–66, 68–69, 71
Trojan Women, 75–76

Ulysses, 16, 21, 54, 75–76, 105–107
Unlevelling effect, 86
Un perro andaluz, 66

Valverde, José María, 85, 106
Vega, Lope de, 84, 87
Velázquez, Diego, 84
Vygotsky, Lev Semo'onovich, 2, 8, 23

Wagner, Richard K., 6
Wall, 2, 12, 32–33, 62, 44–45, 48–49, 52–53, 58, 93, 116
Weber, Max, 17, 23
Wechsler, David, 8
What Is to Be Done?, 98–99
Willis, Paul E., 2, 12
Wittgenstein, Ludwig, 4

Zola, Émile, 38, 42–43

About the Author

Ramón Flecha is professor of sociology and director of the Center for Social and Educational Research, Universitat de Barcelona, Spain. He has published extensively on education and critical social theory, including *Critical Education in the New Information Age* (with Michael Castells, Paulo Freire, Donaldo Macedo, Henry A. Giroux, and Paul Willis, Rowman & Littlefield, 1999) and "Modern & Postmodern Racism: Dialogic Approach and Anti-Racist Pedagogies," (1999) published in *Harvard Educational Review*.